Making Disciples
in Oregon

C. F. SWANDER, B.A., M.A.
State Secretary Oregon Christian Missionary Convention

1928

DEDICATION

In appreciation of the earnest and loyal devotion of the many men who have served with me upon the State Missionary Board for the past twenty years, giving of their time and service without recompense in caring for the things of the kingdom, and who have never in all these years given to their Secretary an unkind or harsh criticism, but who have diligently sustained him and made his task as light as possible at all times, this volume is lovingly dedicated to their memory.

C. F. SWANDER.

FOREWORD

Many years ago the author was told that he should write a book. He has hesitated to enter the field of literature because of the decided conviction that the issuance of a new book is justified only under certain considerations. A new book should add something to the sum total of human knowledge; or, it should state old facts in a sufficiently new way by which they may be more readily grasped or retained; or, it should bring together data that would otherwise be inaccessible to those interested. The only justification the author claims for the appearance of this volume is the last consideration. There is no other History of the Churches of Christ in Oregon. Regardless of its literary merit it will have in its favor the fact that it is entering an entirely new field, and is doing a work for oncoming generations that no one else has hitherto attempted. When the work was begun it was with many misgivings. The time for its composition must be taken out of an already filled program. The source of material was meager and the possible avenues of research were getting scantier every year. It was undertaken in the hope that it might be a contribution to the cause of primitive Christianity, to the promulgation of Christian unity, and to the evangelization of the state of Oregon.

THE AUTHOR.

CONTENTS

CHAPTER VI

CHAPTER VII

CHAPTER VIII

CHAPTER IX

CHAPTER X

CHAPTER XI

CONTENTS

INTRODUCTION

The history of the church, properly understood, is one of the most fascinating of all studies. Dealing as it does with God's leading and man's response to His divine call, it has a charm far above any secular history, and an inspiration that only comes through a better knowledge of the progress of the kingdom of Christ on earth.

It has recently been said by a certain writer that "the most useful books are books of history and biography." I do not know how near to the truth this is, nor do I know that it would be the conclusion of a large number of students and writers; but of this I am certain, that among the books which are contributing to the good of the world there are none that live longer, nor bless the world more abundantly, than books of carefully written history.

The field of the early history of the church apparently has been well covered. It is just as apparent, however, that today when history is being made faster than ever before we are neglecting to record the progress of the church, and to preserve the names of those who, by their sacrifices, have laid a foundation for our present standing and future greatness.

The history and traditions of the Disciples of Christ in Oregon afford us information of which we are justly proud. Yet the time has come when such history must be preserved or it will pass forever from the knowledge of future generations. It is with this idea in mind that the author of this excellent work has given us a most careful and comprehensive history of the Disciples of Christ in Oregon.

Mr. C. F. Swander, the author, has been a resident of Oregon for a quarter of a century, and twenty years of that time have been given over to the office of State Missionary Secretary which has made him the leader in the missionary work of the state. Because of these years of service and his constant contact with the churches there is no man in the state who knows the history of the Church of Christ better and who is more familiar with the work of the Restoration Movement, nor who is better qualified to write such a book, than is he.

It is very important that the names of those who have had such an important part in the development of our work as a people should be preserved. We owe it to their memory, and we owe it to future generations, to have their inspiring services recorded. Neglect on the part of someone qualified for this service has been almost too long, until the years have passed, the pioneers have gone to their reward, and we do not have the story of their lives of sacrifice. It is indeed fortunate that the author of this book had the prophetic vision to see the importance of such a volume and has made this contribution to the brotherhood.

Mr. Swander has given us a great production. It is great because it is timely; it is great because it deals with a people who have been mighty in their missionary and evangelistic zeal; it is great because it gives a picture of great souls, the pioneers of the Church of Christ, who stood for new ideas and a new movement and who inaugurated a definite purpose to return to New Testament Christianity which meant the unity of the people of God on the Bible and the Bible alone.

The author of this volume is a careful student, an excellent writer, a successful leader in missionary and evangelistic work, and, best of all, a faithful preacher of the gospel. He is prepared educationally as well as by experience to write such a book. This product of his heart and his brain will preserve the history of the church and her leaders, and it will be remembered in years to come as a needed contribution to our constantly growing literature. It will enrich many lives who will thank the author for his generous contribution of inspiration and joy as well as knowledge to their lives through this volume.

E. V. STIVERS,
President State Board,
Pastor First Church, Eugene.

Eugene, Oregon.

CHAPTER I

FOUNDATION BUILDERS

When a lad in the district school upon the rolling prairies of Iowa the name "Oregon" was always associated with a patch of green upon a far corner of the map of the United States. To me, green was synonymous with the pleasures of summer time—the shade of trees, the swimming pool, games, etc. It seemed, therefore, that Oregon must be a place of perpetual summer. It was the one spot on the map that was a lure to my imagination.

The Oregon of today is vastly different from the territory that originally bore the name. The name is first found in history in the published works of Captain Jonathan Carver in 1768. It was there applied to a river—the river now bearing the name *Columbia*. Bryant has immortalized the name in "Thanatopsis" with the phrase, "where rolls the Oregon," also referring to that river. It is impossible to know at just what date the name began to be applied to the country. The origin of the name is clouded in hopeless obscurity and it is outside the purpose of this treatise to discuss theoretic origins. The earliest references apply it to all that territory from the Rocky Mountains to the Pacific Ocean, and from Mexico to the Aurora Borealis. In due time California came to be a place to itself, and Oregon then became the great Northwest. As the country increased in commercial importance this region was finally divided between the United States and Great Britain. That part south of the British boundary was carved up into many commonwealths, while the present state of Oregon has retained the name and the glory.

The earliest inhabitants of Oregon were a miscellaneous collection of Indian tribes, having little or no political affiliation, speaking different languages and dialects, and often warring among themselves. It is estimated that in the early part of the nineteenth century there were about 100,000 Indians in the states now known as Oregon, Washington, Idaho and Montana. Today there is probably not one-fifth that number. These primeval tribes are best immortalized by the Indian names in our geography. There we find Multnomah, Tillamook, Clatsop, Yamhill, Calapooia, Umpqua, Coos, Wasco, Klickitat, Umatilla, Klamath, Cayuse, Nez Perces, Walla Walla, and many others.

The Indian is by nature a worshipful creature. He does not readily reason from cause to effect, but he does reason from an effect to a cause. Hence, when any untoward circumstance arose in his experience for which there was not an easily discerned reason, his spiritual nature, adulterated with superstition, ascribed it to the direct operation of spirits. When sickness broke out in an Indian school they attributed the sickness to an evil spell cast upon their children by the white man. This tendency was a most serious handicap to the progress of Christian civilization. The American Indian has been, perhaps, the most difficult subject that Christian Missions has had to deal with. Notwithstanding this there were many splendid examples of spiritual conquest among the original inhabitants of this coast.

It was the Indian's spiritual longing that beckoned the church to the Northwest. The story is a wonderfully thrilling one, equal in sublimity and significance to the vision of "the man of Macedonia" that came to Paul centuries ago. Far up in the mountain fastnesses of the Northwest in 1832 the Indians heard strange tales from wandering trappers of a wonderful book the white man possessed. To these red skinned children of the forest it was the "Book of Heaven." Their spiritual longing was stronger than their lust for blood. This book was their theme at council meetings, and, at last, they determined to search it out. Selecting an old sachem and three young braves they sent them on the long, long trail to Fort St. Louis, then only a fur traders' post on the frontier, to ask for this wonderful book. Many weeks later they arrived at the fort. They were received kindly, and were fêted and banqueted as royal guests; but when they made known the object of their quest they only met with disappointment. Finally two of them sickened and died. At last, after many weeks of fruitless search, broken hearted and disappointed, the other two prepared to return to their people. Before going they immortalized the incident in words as follows:

"We came to you over a trail of many moons from the setting sun. You were the friend of our Fathers who have all gone the long way. We came with our eyes partly opened for more light for our people who sit in darkness. We go back with our eyes closed. How can we go back with our eyes blind to our blind people? We made our way to you with strong arms, through many enemies and strange lands, that we might carry back much to them. We go back with empty and broken arms. The two fathers who came with us—the braves of many winters and wars—we leave them here asleep by your great wigwam. They were tired in their journey of many moons, and their moccasins were worn out.

"Our people sent us to get the white man's Book of Heaven. You took us to where they worship the Great Spirit with candles, but the Book was not there. You showed us the images of good spirits, and pictures of the good land beyond, but the Book was not among them to tell us the way. You made our feet heavy with the burden of gifts, and our moccasins will grow old with the carrying of them, but the Book is not among them. We are going back the long, sad trail to our people. When we tell them, after one more snow, in the big council, that we did not bring the Book, no word will be spoken by our old men, nor by our young braves. One by one they will rise up and go out in silence. Our people will die in darkness, and they will go on the long path to other hunting grounds. No white man will go with them, and no Book of Heaven to make the way plain. We have no more words.''

Sadly they went on their way. Only one reached his people to report the sad failure of their mission. The newspapers published the story. Jason Lee, a native of East Canada and recently ordained to the Methodist ministry in the New England states, read the account. His soul was stirred. Alive with youthful vigor and imagination he quickly saw in it an opportunity for the church in missionary enterprise. He besought the Missionary Board with much entreaty to assist him in a mission to the Flathead Indians. They yielded and he raised a company of five families for the trip. Though destined for the home of the Flatheads, which was in what is now Idaho, they did not stop until they reached the Oregon territory and the Willamette Valley. This was in the year 1834. There were probably not more than a dozen American settlers in Oregon at that time.

The earliest history of civilization in Oregon was a combination of political and religious. The Hudson's Bay Company, with headquarters on the Columbia River where Vancouver now stands, was an English fur trading corporation. Their commerce was in the unbroken wilds. Civilization would interfere with trapping, therefore they were opposed to the settlement of the country. Missionaries encouraged the settlement of the country, therefore they were opposed to missionaries. Discouraging reports concerning the country were sent East. Settlers were "advised" to move up the valley. The company owned all the cattle in the country and refused to sell to the settlers. This made it exceedingly difficult to develop the country.

Dr. John McLoughlin was the Superintendent of Hudson's Bay Company. Though connected with a "soulless" corporation, Dr. McLoughlin possessed a soul—very large and of exceedingly fine texture. Though compelled to *enforce* the rules of the company he found many ways of assisting the settlers, and in doing so he manifested a big humanitarianism. When "advising" settlers to move on he furnished conveyance, provisions, and help to move, when necessary; and, when unable to sell them cattle, he helped to organize a company to drive a herd from California, and even furnished most of the money to buy the cattle.

Associated with Hudson's Bay Company at Vancouver were some Jesuit priests. They used their influence against American immigration to the country. As late as 1840 there were only about 114 Americans of all ages in the Willamette Valley. The Hudson's Bay Company adherents were about the same number. The political contest between English and American sovereignty was, therefore, quite evenly divided. For many months the question of sovereignty was hotly discussed. The British feared the Americans would out-vote them if it was settled by a plebiscite, so they started a movement for a free and independent government in Oregon. The Americans feared that if the question were put to a vote in that form it might carry; but they believed a straight vote on American sovereignty would win.

Jason Lee, the missionary, was more than a missionary—he was a statesman. He reached Oregon in 1834 when there was only a handful of Americans in the whole land. He saw the gathering political storm, with the clouds of political intrigue and the lightnings of political hatred. His statesman's soul caught a vision of the significance of this western land for the future and he coveted it for the land of his adoption. After witnessing all these things for four years he determined to go east for reinforcements. Accordingly in 1838 he crossed the continent, laid before President Van Buren a plea and a plan to aid settlers in Oregon, and then organized a company of immigrants for the western journey.

Lee returned to the Willamette Valley in 1840. Three years later the vote on sovereignty took place. On May 2, 1843, the matter came to a head at a mass meeting of the settlers. While the English were trying to bring a vote on independent government, Joe Meek, trapper and mountaineer, suddenly and without warning, sprang to one side and cried out,

"All in favor of American sovereignty, follow me!" The meeting was divided. A majority of two followed Meek. It was a victory, not only for America, but for protestantism as well. If the English propaganda had won Roman Catholicism would doubtless have had ascendency in the state of Oregon to this day.

While these things were being enacted in the Willamette Valley, Marcus Whitman, a missionary at Fort Walla Walla across the mountains to the east, was helping the political fortunes of American sovereignty there. Overhearing a remark made by a priest in the fort one day Whitman concluded that the British were contemplating an immigration to the territory. Immediately his resolve was made. He would go back to the States, interest Congress, and return with an immigration sufficient to make the territory secure for the United States. Although it was then late in October, within three days he was in the saddle and starting on a 2,500 mile journey across trackless mountains and desert plains. One companion started with him, but the rigors of the journey compelled him to turn back. Picking up a Mexican guide he pushed on. The guide froze to death. Led by the instincts of his mule Whitman succeeded in crossing the mountains and in March following he reached Fort St. Louis. He pressed on immediately to Washington where he laid his plan before the Secretary of State, Daniel Webster. That worthy statesman was not impressed. Whitman sought President Tyler and begged him to rescind the treaty of joint occupation with England, to extend the jurisdiction of the United States over the territory of Oregon, and to offer financial inducements to emigrants to go to the Northwest. President Tyler was deeply impressed, and in consequence Marcus Whitman had the pleasure and honor of leading a train of 1,000 immigrants to Oregon during the summer of 1843. Most of them went on through to the Willamette Valley, and they arrived while the settlers were still in controversy over the vote forced by Meek in May before. The American population was now so tremendously in the majority that the question of sovereignty was forever settled.

Marcus Whitman's ride across the continent and the immigration he led back is generally credited with being the salvation of Oregon for the United States. It may have been the great decisive factor. But it must not be forgotten that Jason Lee's trip was a full five years earlier, and that it had the same objective, and resulted in the same attainment though in a lesser degree. The story of Lee's trip has not been embellished with adventure, hardship and danger as was Whitman's though doubtless there was just as much of each. Whitman had more apparent results from his trip than did Lee; but there is some question whether he would have been so successful had it not been for the breaking of the trail by Lee before him.

Lee was not satisfied with the results of 1843. Accordingly he left again that year for another trip east in the interest of political sovereignty. He laid before Congress, as Whitman had done, the expediency of terminating the treaty with England which provided for joint occupancy of the land, and to establish American laws and institutions there. While on this trip he was taken ill and died, never again to see the Oregon land in the West which he loved.

Aside from Dr. John McLoughlin the two great characters of early Oregon were Marcus Whitman and Jason Lee. Both died for the land they loved—Whitman a martyr to the savage tomahawk; Lee a martyr to labors too heavy for his constitution. Of the two, however, Lee was the more an Oregonian for he was in the center of its early development in a way that Whitman was not, and could not be. Oregon may then be pardoned for honoring him more highly than the others. It was the Methodist Conference that transferred his body, 60 years after his death, from the native soil in which it was first buried, to Oregon soil, its legitimate resting place. On June 15, 1906, it was planted with fitting ceremony in the Lee Mission Cemetery at Salem, Oregon. It matters not much where a man's body shall lie after his death; but there is a tender sentiment attached to some characters, and it is all the greater tribute to both the Methodist Church, and to the state of Oregon, that they should desire Lee's body than it is to himself. The memorial address at the reinterment was given by Harvey W. Scott, then editor of the *Morning Oregonian* (Portland, Oregon), a thorough student of Oregon history and a great admirer of Jason Lee. In that address he paid this tribute:

"It was not until the American missionaries entered and possessed the country that a foothold was gained for the occupation of Oregon by American settlers."

It was a tribute alike to Jason Lee and to the church; and it carries all the more significance when we stop to recall that Mr. Scott was rather skeptical, at least very liberal in religious thought, at that time. His editorials were constantly flavored with such periods. Mr. Scott attributes to Jason Lee more than to any other the credit for Oregon becoming an American state.

Not only did Lee lay the foundations of a political commonwealth in Oregon, but they were foundations of a *Christian* commonwealth. Therefore, it is not surprising that Oregon has always been in the vanguard of moral reform, that she was one of the first states in the union to outlaw liquor, that the church here has always been an influential factor in civic problems, that Christian education has always had a distinct place in Oregon's history, and that the public schools have had their most loyal supporters here. This is not a chance condition, nor does it mean that Oregon has been more led of God than other states; but it does tell that early foundations were securely laid.

It may seem that we are giving Jason Lee undue credit for Oregon's political and religious fabric. But it is only seemingly so. Without doubt the major credit for those early beginnings belongs to him. Lee was sent to Oregon by the Methodist Missionary Board; but his labors were as undenominational as they could well be. Nor does the Methodist Church share alone the fruitage of his life. All churches now share alike in that. A great man can belong to one sect only during his generation; after that all sects alike share in the goodness of his career, and increasingly is it distributed as the years roll on. We would not contend with the Methodists concerning the name and fame of Jason Lee; but rather would we with them across his grave clasp hands and claim the fruit of his life as a common heritage, for out of his labors we all have reaped abundantly.

Jason Lee died a martyr's death as truly as he who is slaughtered for truth's sake. There may be more glory in dying from a tomahawk than from a fever, yet it all means very much the same; and the fever may have an even greater story to tell than the tomahawk.

To these early characters—McLoughlin, Whitman, Lee—belong the credit for the foundation of the church in Oregon. But foundation laying is not enough. There must be a superstructure or the foundation is laid in vain. The superstructure must be worthy of the foundation. That foundation was laid deep and strong, sufficient to carry a building of many stories. Each generation builds its own story. We are now in about the third generation from those foundation builders, erecting the third story of the superstructure. The first generation builded well;

the second generation builded well; we must build as well also. We must not only build worthy of that which has gone before, but we must build worthy of that which is to come after.

NOTE.—Since the above chapter was written a number of letters have appeared in Oregon newspapers calling in question the essential facts of the vote on American sovereignty and its effect in securing Oregon territory for the Union. The writer can see no just ground for discrediting the story which appears in the early writings of Oregon's beginnings. It is therefore retained as history.

CHAPTER II

PIONEER DAYS

The political history of Oregon begins properly with May 2, 1843, the day when Joe Meek forced a plebiscite on American sovereignty. The history of the Christian Church in Oregon may properly be said to begin the same year, though some months later, when the first immigration from the states reached the Willamette Valley. The population of the territory was increased by more than 1,000 by this immigration.

There is no historical record that we have yet found that makes mention of Disciples of Christ in that immigration. But it is unbelievable that a train of 1,000 people could come from the state of Missouri, a state where the Christian Church was strong even in that early day, without having members of this religious body in it. A few are known however to have been in it.

Peter H. Burnett was one who is known to have united with the Christian Church in Missouri. After coming to Oregon he read the debate which had taken place in 1837 between Alexander Campbell and Bishop Purcell on the respective merits of Protestantism and Roman Catholicism. As a result he was converted to the Catholic faith and remained a consistent member of that church until his death. He afterwards became governor of California.

Wayman C. Hembree, and a girl who afterwards became his wife, were in that train. The author lived in their home at McMinnville for several months and enjoyed the tales of pioneer days at their fireside. They were only children at the time of the immigration, but became life long members of the Christian Church during the evangelistic fervor of the early days.

William H. Wilson was also in that train. His descendants are among us yet until this day.

Were the full truth known we would doubtless have a considerable list of disciples in that first immigration of 1843. Without question, too, there are many disciples today who could trace their blood lineage back to that caravan, but whose present religious ancestry began much later.

The year 1844 yields no records that are of historical interest to disciples. But the year 1845 brought the first known Christian preachers to Oregon. All of them did great credit and honor to the faith they represented.

Amos Harvey is worthy of first mention in this list because to him belongs the honor of establishing the first Christian Church in the state. When he first arrived in 1845 he spent considerable time seeking a desirable location. Finally he settled "on the banks of the Yamhill River." The court records locate his donation land claim in Polk county. From a letter to the Millennial Harbinger it would seem that the exact location of a dwelling place was occasioned by the fact that he found a few families of disciples scattered through this section. This would seem almost positive proof that there had been "Christians only" in that caravan of 1843. According to his report in the Harbinger he organized a church "on the banks of the Yamhill River" in March, 1846. In that report he said that he had organized a congregation "upon the Book alone—and this was the first congregation built upon this foundation in the territory. We numbered at first but 13 members. We met, as the disciples anciently did, upon the

first day of the week, to break the loaf, to implore assistance of the Heavenly Father, and to encourage each other
in the heavenly way." There is nothing to identify the
exact location of this church. It doubtless was in the home
of one of its faithful members, perhaps the home of Amos
Harvey himself.

John Foster was another worthy in that train of 1845.
He settled on the Clackamas River. That would be a vague
designating term in these days; but then it could not have
been far removed from the present town of Gladstone. He
had no more than "pitched his tent" than he began to
search out scattered disciples among the few inhabitants.
The fact that he found a few would be another evidence
that there were disciples in the train of 1843. Like Amos
Harvey he organized them into a church. But it must
have been some time subsequent to that other "on the
banks of the Yamhill," for Harvey specifically says that
his was the first one in the territory. Presumably Foster
made his organization in the fall after Harvey had made
his in March. Foster continued to preach for this church
until he was an old man. When he finally gave up preaching he could talk for only a few minutes at a time. This
church went the way of human kind. It died, i.e., the
human organization perished and was forgotten. But even
as there is a spirit in man that goes back to God who gave
it, so the spirit of this church has gone down the stream of
time; and no man knows to this day how much he owes
in a spiritual way to that old, forgotten church on the
Clackamas.

H. M. Waller was another preacher in that caravan of
1845. He was from Illinois. Timid and retiring by nature
on ordinary occasions, when he stood before an audience

and exhorted sinners to repent, his timidity fled and he
was a veritable giant. It has been said of him that he
made more converts than any other preacher this country
ever had. (Of course we must remember that the comparison does not cover the last three-score years). We
have found many of our older brethren who knew Waller
personally and they have invariably spoken loving words
in memory of him. The old church at Eola, recently razed
to the ground, was the product of his preaching.

We have the record of five preachers whose coming
can be traced to the year 1846. First, and most prominent,
was Glen O. Burnett, a brother to Peter H. Burnett who
had come in 1843 and had afterwards defected to Roman
Catholicism. He was a Tennesseean by birth. He settled
on a donation land claim of 640 acres east of the present
town of McCoy, in Polk county. He gave the name
"Bethel Hills" to the heights adjoining, which name they
carry to this day. The name was given in memory of the
old Bethel church for which he had preached in Missouri.
The church afterwards organized on his place became the
"Bethel Church," and was so known until it closed its
doors forever in comparatively recent years. He was a
deep thinker and a strong pulpiteer. With strong logic
and in scathing terms he denounced sin. Sectarianism
and division burdened his soul. It was in strictest rever-
ence that he would cry out as if in despair over religious
conditions, "O, if I only had the strength I would knock
the gable end out of sectarianism." The strength, yet
tenderness, of his appeal was almost irresistible, and it is
said that he gave but few invitations without responses
from penitent souls. His home was a haven for passing
disciples, and he always guided the conversation by the

fireside into the great themes of the Bible. He preached
his last sermon in the old Bethany church near Silverton.
Being too weak to stand he sat while preaching. The congregation was visibly affected and many wept.

Dr. James McBride is assigned to the year 1846. We
have found but little recorded concerning this man, but
it is known that he settled in Yamhill county and from
him came a long line of citizens who have occupied chief
places in councils of state. Though primarily a physician
he was a preacher as opportunity offered and pastored
some of the early, struggling congregations.

Elijah Bristow is another preacher known to have been
in the immigration of 1846. He settled in Lane county,
and was one of the founders of the Pleasant Hill Church,
a country congregation that bears an enviable record. He
led the immigrant train to the top of an eminence in Lane
county and stopped. Looking around upon the beautiful
prospect he exclaimed, ''This is Pleasant Hill. Here will
I live, here will I die, and here will I be buried.'' It was
even so. The community is known as Pleasant Hill to this
day. Elijah Bristow sleeps in the cemetery on that hill,
and his picture hangs on the wall of the little church hard
by. A numerous progeny perpetuate the name of so worthy
an ancestor. The family has contributed materially to the
development of the state both politically and religiously.

The caravan of 1846 brought a lad of four years who
was destined to become one of Oregon's most honored
preachers—Peter R. Burnett, a son of Glen O. Burnett,
and a nephew of Peter H. Burnett. He was the last one
of those early pioneer preachers to ''go home.'' He im-
bibed an early desire for the ministry. His mother was
a ''Hannah'' and his father taught him ''the law.'' His

education was achieved under truly pioneer conditions. In the academy at Lafayette sessions were held in an "upper room" not like the one of Pentecostal days, but a room above a saloon. But even the proximity of malt spirits could not quench the thirsting for the divine Spirit in young Peter. He afterwards attended school at Bethel Institute (near the present town of McCoy), and later at Hesperian College in Woodland, California. He was one of the first of the pioneer preachers to give himself wholly to the ministry of the Word. It had been the custom of the pioneer preachers to make their living at farming and preach on Sundays; but Peter launched out into the deep and trusted the apostolic decision that "they who preach the gospel shall live of the gospel." Sometimes the support was small and he was called upon to endure privation; but he had put his hand to the plow and he did not look back. When out of a job he went out and made a place for himself. As a result he established many new churches and baptized more than 2000 converts. When there was no other way of going to his appointments he walked. "When asked if, knowing what he now knows, he had his life to live over again, he would choose the life of a minister, his answer was always, 'Yes, though with my present experience I would certainly avoid some of the mistakes which I am conscious of having made.'" Brother Burnett's end was an untimely one. On November 9, 1922, while on his way home from prayer meeting in Eugene he was struck by an automobile and sustained injuries from which he died a few days later. He was the last one of the pioneer preachers. Even after closing his active ministry he preached with fervor, and the sparkle of his eye was a reflection of the greatness of his soul.

He was one preacher who accepted "retirement" gracefully. No "grouch" ever spoiled the beauty of his soul. No jealousy ever marred his relationship with his fellow preachers. It is one of the fond memories of the author that for a period he was the pastor of this great and good man, and for this privilege he will always be thankful. His presence in the audience was always a benediction; his visits to the study were always helpful; his counsel was always good. If it should seem that overmuch space is devoted to this one character in proportion to others it may be accounted for, and justified by, the author's personal relationship to him.

The year 1846 claims the organization of Yamhill county's first church. "The first church organized in Yamhill county was in School District No. 1, August 1, 1846, by Vincent Snelling, on the Ruel Olds place. The first man baptized by immersion was in the Yamhill River, just below the Andy Hembree place, on Sunday, August 2, 1846. The man baptized was Wm. Higgins, a son-in-law of V. Snelling."—From a letter by F. M. York, who claims to have received this information from G. L. Rowland who was present at the organization. We have checked back the dates and find that August 1, 1846 did fall on Saturday. There is nothing further in the records about this church.

The year 1847 yields but one item of interest—the organization of the church that today must be recognized as the oldest living Christian Church in the state. In that year 14 disciples met in the Blackhawk schoolhouse, six miles northwest of the present site of McMinnville, and were organized by Aaron Payne into a Church of Christ. Six years later the congregation moved to within a mile

and a half of town to the Shaddon schoolhouse. In 1855
the church home was moved to McMinnville. This church
has had a great record. The author was its pastor for
three years and seven months.

The year 1848 yields one scanty item—the organization
of a church at Damascus, in Clackamas county. The year
1849 is totally blank so far as can be discovered from historical data. But we doubt not that both years were over-
flowing with goodness. Disciples have always been too
busy making history to record it. That is perhaps the
reason why these two years are so scantily preserved in
history.

1850 gives several items of interest. In this year the
Bethany church was organized, in Marion county, near
Silverton. A building was erected in 1858 which is still
standing in a very good state of repair, and is now the
oldest standing Christian Church building in the state.
The inscription, ''Bethany Christian Church, Erected in
1858,'' is still visible, and in its silent way is still preaching the way to heaven. The old cemetery about the building was, for a long time, left to decay. Vandals had torn
away the gravestones leaving graves unidentified and impossible to locate. In 1927 interested persons repaired and
restored the cemetery as much as it was possible to do.

It was this year that gave to Oregon Sebastian Adams, a
pioneer teacher of prominence and power. He was one of
the first settlers of McMinnville, and helped to organize
McMinnville College, at that time a Christian Church
school. For many years he ministered at Salem.

Elijah B. Davidson is another name that belongs to this
year. He took up a donation land claim in what is now
known as East Portland. He later moved to Polk county,

from whence he went to Josephine county, where he died in 1888. All up and down the valley he preached the gospel in that pioneer day.

The most interesting item for this year is the organization of the church at Pleasant Hill, on August 4, 1850, some 12 miles southeast of Eugene, in Lane county. It was a purely rural spot, and the place was appropriately named. It was upon the hill where Elijah Bristow had paused four years before. This church is one of the few purely rural congregations that has maintained an uninterrupted existence through a long period of years. Elijah Bristow wrote to the Millennial Harbinger concerning it as follows: ''We copied, as a heading to our Church Book, a preamble and agreement from the Millennial Harbinger at the time of organizing. Only one man made any objection, but he finally subscribed his name to it. His objection was, he thought it longer than necessary.'' Heresy hunting and faultfinding are evidently not confined to our own day.

1851 gives many interesting and important items. Among them was the advent of three brothers, all preachers —John, Alfred, and Noah Powell. They settled in Linn County and preached wherever opportunity offered. If an opportunity did not offer itself they made one. John and Alfred usually went together. John was the preacher while Alfred led the song and gave the exhortation. The sermon would be from 45 minutes to an hour in length, after which Alfred would address the audience with an impassioned exhortation. The invitation song would then be sung and it was a rare occasion when sinners did not confess their Lord. In 1852 John Powell ''became the first missionary of the Christian Church in Oregon, and

travelled horseback the length of the state, establishing
churches, and sowing the seed for future religious work. . . .
He was six feet in height, and weighed 225 pounds. . . . His
commanding appearance, his strong, clear voice, and his
logic and magnetism easily enabled him to hold the un-
divided attention of his audience for an hour and often
much longer. . . . He was of a serious turn of mind, and
seldom indulged in a jest. In contrast to the fiery ex-
hortations of his brother Alfred, his public discourses were
quiet and dignified in style; his manner of speaking was
deliberate. His sermons did not call for great demonstra-
tions, but were designed to give men food for serious
thought concerning the great issues of life.''

1851 also brought an interesting and lovable character
in the person of J. V. Crawford. He was a lad of 12 years
when he arrived in Yamhill county from St. Joseph, Missouri, via ox team. It took five months to make the journey. He himself writes concerning the journey as follows:

"My parents, who were then in the prime of their lives, being
on the sunny side of forty, were very earnest and devout disciples.
. . . . One of the first things they did after reaching their destina-
tion was to take a kind of religious census of the community to discover if there were any of their own faith and order. The results
were highly gratifying. They were upon all sides of us.''

In due time Brother Crawford became a preacher of the
Word. His footprints are still seen, especially east of the
mountains where he served most of his ministry. He is
another one of the pioneers whom it was the privilege of
the author to know personally; and out of that acquaint-
ance has grown the conviction that if there are any seats
in heaven higher and easier than others Brother Crawford will be occupying one of them.

1851 yields a generous list of names whom we can mention only briefly. John E. Murphey came from Illinois in a company of disciples whose main object was to build a religious school in Oregon. In the East he had been associated with the Restoration Fathers. He was a great exhorter. He was Vice President and Financial Secretary of Monmouth College until his death in 1876.

John Rigdon was a cousin to Sidney Rigdon, of Mormon fame. He had studied under Alexander Campbell, and was associated with Walter Scott, Barton W. Stone, John T. Smith, John T. Johnson, etc. He knew the Book and preached it with great power.

Gilmore Callison came from Illinois this year and settled in Lane county. A preacher in Illinois, he remained a preacher in Oregon. He had the honor of organizing the church in Eugene, which has since grown to be the largest Christian Church in the state, and one of the greatest on the Pacific coast. He was a member of the state legislature in 1864-65.

Rufus G. Callison was a son of Gilmore Callison. As a lad of 13 he crossed the plains. With the exception of a few months he never lived outside of Lane county. Much of his preaching was done in connection with teaching school. His death was a beautiful ending of an active life. While delivering an address at the state convention at Turner on July 7, 1915, he paused a moment, rested heavily upon the desk, and while his spirit took its flight his body sunk gently to the floor. It was as he would have wished—he died in the harness.

Other names are ascribed to the period before 1860 but without certainty as to date. A. V. McCarty was said to have had a wonderful memory, a musical voice, and could preach for two hours without tiring his hearers. Wm. L.

Adams was a graduate of Oberlin College, and ordained as a Cumberland Presbyterian preacher; but, accepting the Restoration plea, he went to Bethany and sat at the feet of Alexander Campbell. A. R. Elder was a fluent speaker. He afterwards joined the Presbyterians. John Nelson Perkins was both a preacher and a physician. He engaged in business and politics. Other men, of whom we can get little data beyond the fact that they were in the forefront of the "good fight of faith," are as follows: George W. Richardson, James R. Fisher, Philip Mulkey, L. L. Rowland, Charles Bradshaw, E. G. Browning, Elder Casteel, W. T. Haley, Joel Vail, S. Y. Bailey, Samuel Briggs, and Elder Trollinger.

The year 1864 yields data of an interesting character in the person of Martin Petterson, who crossed the plains and settled in the Sacramento Valley in 1863, coming to Oregon a year later. To him belongs the honor of organizing the first Christian Church in southern Oregon. He built the first schoolhouse in his part of the state at his own expense and preached in it until his death. To his labors are indebted the churches of Medford, Ashland and Central point. Other churches were organized by him in Jackson and Josephine counties which did not endure. His zeal for the cause was evidenced by the fact that in crossing the plains he held services regularly every Lord's Day with the emigrant train. He called it the "First Church on Wheels." There were 30 members of the Christian Church in that train. While preaching a sermon on June 30, 1889, he was stricken down and died the next day. He devoted his entire life to the church and steadfastly refused ever to take a penny for his labors.

1865 brought John M. Harris to Oregon and who was a prominent figure in Christian work for many years. Born in Kentucky in 1803 he preached in Indiana and Illinois during his early years. He served as evangelist in the states of California, Oregon and Washington. He was pastor at Albany, Pleasant Hill and Cottage Grove. He helped to dedicate the old brick church in Eugene together with Rufus Callison and Uncle Philip Mulkey. He believed what he preached and did not hesitate to preach what he believed. At times he "had a great deal to say about how the South was abused." Those were the days, it must be remembered, when the Mason and Dixon line radiated out like spokes from a hub! Old residents still remember him as "reading his text, taking off his glasses, and preaching for an hour with all the power and earnestness he could command." He passed on in 1881 after living to see the cause he so dearly loved well established.

A. L. Todd was a pioneer of somewhere in the '60s. He lived in Looking Glass Valley and preached through Douglas county as he had opportunity. He worked and preached at the Cinnabar Mines in Shoestring Valley. We find in the reports the notice of a church at Shoestring Valley in 1900. This was a much later date than Todd preached, but one can legitimately conclude that his preaching was the seed sowing that reaped a harvest later. He was called to his reward in Eugene, and his faithful wife, for long familiarly known as "Grandma Todd" was the first inmate of the Old People's Home established at Eugene in 1906 and later moved to Walla Walla. She died at the latter place.

Of these pioneer preachers one of their own number speaks a deserved tribute:

"These were all genuine missionaries of the cross, and their time and labors were a voluntary contribution to the cause they loved with a sublime devotion. There were no missionary societies behind them to direct their labors or pay their salaries: but, like Paul of old, they worked with their own hands that they might not be burdensome to any. There was not even concerted action between themselves. All was chaos so far as organization was concerned. Had they been able to look a little further into the future, and to have shaken off completely the nightmare of what is now known as anti-ism, the cause for which they so ably plead and at so great a sacrifice, would now be fifty years in advance of where it is. But they were great and good men and did a mighty work for God. Their names are among the immortals, and their memory should be embalmed in the heart of every true Disciple in the great Northwest.''—From the private correspondence of J. V. Crawford.

Amen!

Another able eulogium of the work of the minister of that day, bordering with much justice on a critique of modern times, is furnished from the pen of H. C. Porter, a son of a pioneer preacher, and still to this day a pillar in the Aumsville church:

"Some may imagine the preaching of those days was the backwoods style delivered by ministers lacking in Bible knowledge. But such was not the case. Their Bible knowledge would compare favorably with that of our best ministers today. In fact, they had to more earnestly contend for the faith which was once and for all delivered to the saints, for they met with more opposition in those days than do our ministers of the present time. The title, or prefix, Rev. was never used. We would often hear them spoken of as 'Brother,' or 'Uncle.' They seldom, if ever, announced beforehand the subject of their sermon. This was before the time of announcing catchy, or sensational subjects for sermons, a fad which at the present time has gone to seed. This reminds me of a young man who came to us less than a hundred years ago, fresh from school, and after preaching a few sermons announced that on a certain evening he would preach the funeral of the Aumsville Christian Church. When the time arrived, no doubt believing that standing room would be at a premium, he was on hand early and tolled the bell. When the audience arrived and he found there were not enough present to act as pall bearers, the sermon was indefinitely postponed and the church is still unburied."

The identity of the funeral preacher is not a matter of history.

CHAPTER III

PIONEER PROGRESS

We of the present day can scarcely appreciate the labors of the early pioneers. They did not have the advantages we have in the modern conveniences. Until 1859 there was no train service into the state. The ox team was the "Overland Train and Pullman De Luxe" of those days. The only comfortable means of ingress was the boat via Cape Horn—a long, tedious sea voyage of many months. Nor were there automobiles to whisk one back and forth across the valley between dinner and supper. It required days to make a trip between two points that now require but a few hours. The most common means of transportation was a cayuse. If the preacher was so fortunate as to possess one he rode; if not, he walked. "Shanks horses" were always ready and willing. They brooked no difficulties in meeting appointments. Storm and flood did not deter them. After working six days in the field a preacher would walk nine or ten miles on Sunday morning, preach at 11 o'clock and again at 3 o'clock, then walk home —an utterly impossible thing in these days. But there were giants in those days—giants in hardened muscles, giants in faith, giants in preaching the Word. They were unhampered with classical learning, yet some of them could read the Greek New Testament more readily than most of the moderns. Their libraries consisted of a few, but well chosen, books. Above all else they knew the Word, and preached it. As a consequence the waters were often troubled—with baptisms. Few religious opponents could withstand them in debate. A prominent ecclesiastic once exclaimed in dismay, perhaps flavored with anger, "The Campbellites and the fern are taking the Willamette Valley!"

The background is essential to the proper display of a picture. We can best appreciate the growth of the church during pioneer days if we keep before our eyes the physical conditions under which the pioneers lived. We are indebted to a sketch by "Aunt Jane" Powell, of Monmouth, in the book "The Powell Family," for the following background of a picture of the pioneer church:

"The 16th day of September (1851) we reached a suitable stopping place near the Santiam river, and after looking around located on the prairie about seven miles east of Albany. . . . . Our house was sixteen feet square. It was built of hewn logs covered with three-foot boards rived out with a fro, with similar boards nailed over the cracks in the walls. There were two doors. . . . . The house had a rough floor made out of boards split out of fir timber. There was no window, but we would usually keep one door open for light. In the east side were the fireplace and hearth made of rock. The chimney was built of sticks and mud, and was run up on the outside of the wall. Our fire shovel was a board until Pa made one from a piece of iron from an old wagon. Our furniture consisted of trestle benches for a bedstead, home made stools, tables and one chair which we brought with us. . . . We kept house over a year without a cook-stove, or a fireplace irons, or a shovel. Our live stock was a cow until Pa traded his gun for an Indian pony. . . . . Our cooking utensils were: a tea-kettle, coffee pot, frying pan, stew kettle, two pans, and a deep skillet with a lid to bake bread in. . . . . For several years wheat was legal tender, rated at one dollar a bushel. Our first crop of wheat was seven acres put in and threshed out with oxen. The threshing floors were made by smoothing off the ground and pouring water on it, then pounding it with a heavy maul until it was hard. Wheat for bread was flailed out and separated in the wind by pouring it onto a wagon sheet. . . . . It was several years before we got the first team of horses, which Pa helped to pay for by walking three miles to the timber and making rails."

This background of the early church in Oregon is almost identical with the background of the first church in Bible times! Added to these physical hardships was the presence of the Indians, of whom there were many tribes in the valley, hostile to each other and to the whites. Depredations were a frequent occurrence. When a man went away from home he never knew but what he would find smoking ruins and butchered family when he returned. As the country settled these dangers grew less and less until they faded out entirely.

The historical material for this period consists mainly of reports sent to church papers. *The Christian-Evangelist* and the *Millennial Harbinger* were the papers of that early day, published in St. Louis, Missouri, and in Bethany, West Virginia, respectively. It took many weeks to get a church report in the papers, and as many weeks to get the papers back to its readers in Oregon. The reports were disjointed and disconnected. It is impossible to patch them together in a historical narrative without the imaginative element used in fiction. However, it can be easily seen from them that the cause grew rapidly, considering the small population of the territory.

From the three congregations that formed the beginning of the Disciples of Christ in Oregon in 1846—"On the Yamhill," "On the Clackamas," and "In Yamhill county,"—they had increased in 1850 to "six respectable churches, and seven or eight preachers, without pecuniary assistance."—Dr. James McBride.

In 1851 there were "little country organizations here and there over the land."—J. V. Crawford.

In 1852 Glen O. Burnett wrote to the *Millennial Harbinger*: "We have in Oregon about 1,200 disciples, but in a most disorganized condition."

In 1854 Dr. McBride wrote to the *Harbinger*: "I can say with much assurance that the 'Christians' number not

less than 800 in Oregon . . . . and about 20 preachers in
the territory.''

One is struck with the difference in numbers—1,200 in
1852 and 800 in 1854! It may be accounted for by the
fact that there was no statistical machinery in those days,
and reports were necessarily only estimates. There was
no sufficient bond of fellowship in that early day but the
bond of a common faith. Estimates would be based solely
upon the reporter's horizon—if it was broad he saw more;
if it was narrow, he saw less. We are inclined to place
greater credence in Burnett's estimate than in McBride's,
for the reason that Burnett circulated through the valley
more than McBride did, and consequently had a larger
and better basis upon which to pass judgment. But, according to either report, the growth from 13 in March,
1846 to either 800 or 1,200 in 1854 was a wonderful increase.

The spirit of evangelism moved those early pioneers.
There were no secular attractions, or amusements, to dis-
tract the minds of the people. Movies had not yet been in-
vented. Dancing may have been indulged in, but it was not
a mania. Religious meetings were the most common media
for social intercourse. The isolation of the settlers and the
precarious means of travel were almost prohibitive of night
gatherings, and that kept to a minimum those attractions
which love the nighttime best for their performance;
while the gospel thrived in the open day. Consequently
it was easy to get an audience for religious meetings. Nor
were the people of that day content with sermonettes—
they demanded full grown sermons. Those were giant
preachers and they must deliver giant sermons—two and

three hours in length sometimes. The evangelists of that day heard only the voice of the Master, "Go, preach." There were no "settled pastors" as in modern times. Wherever the call was heard it was heeded. Churches were organized wherever convenience dictated. They were not "scientifically" located. Community boundaries were made up largely by topographical characteristics that were real division lines in those days. Hence it was that scores of churches were planted during these, and succeeding, years that have since passed entirely out of existence and some of them out of memory. The demise of these congregations does not indicate a decay of the cause—it was simply an evidence of community development, the shifting of community lines, the introduction of conveniences, the effort of nature to adjust the church to its changing environment.

The news columns of this period read almost like the Acts of the Apostles. A few passages are quoted:

"The Church of Christ here (Pleasant Hill) is now in a flourishing condition. We number some 70 members" (1853).

"Brother Hendrix has baptized some thirty in the vicinity of Hillsborough. We have had 12 additions recently by confession and baptism to this congregation (Lafayette), and 4 by commendation. At South Fork church at two meetings recently, there were 7 additions by confession and obedience. At Bethel near 30 more were added" (1854).

"16 additions by immersion, 29 by letter, 1 reclaimed and 1 from the Baptists" at Spring Valley (1855).

"18 added in meeting at Pleasant Hill" (1855).

"A church organized at Clear Lake, Lane county, on 4th Lord's Day of June, 1855, with 14 members," was soon increased to 39 members.

The spelling of our present day Hillsboro has evoluted downward from 1853! Those early disciples were not ashamed of small beginnings! They did not hesitate to reclaim backsliders and proselyte from the denominations!

These excerpts are typical of scores that can be reproduced, showing the progress of the gospel under pioneer conditions. Yet the hearts of these earnest leaders ached for even greater progress. Discouragement came to those brave souls, though they were undaunted thereby. In 1853 Glen O. Burnett wrote: "I think we are happily emerging, though slowly, from the gloom superinduced by the gold mines of California. . . . In Oregon we have strong opposition; every inch of ground is contested by well disciplined ranks of sectarian preachers whose object, it seems, is to misrepresent those who have renounced all human appendages, and taken the Living Oracles alone."

The Willamette Valley from Pleasant Hill to Portland was the first habitat of this pioneer work. But, like the trees and grasses which spring up in places far removed from their natural habitat, so the church grew out beyond the valley. The far cry of "Come over and help us" was early heard. In 1856 the cry was heard from the Umpqua Valley.

Concerning that call S. D. Evans, located at Winchester, writes: "We have great need of help here. We have no preacher at all in the Umpqua Valley; and a large field lies unoccupied. Will not some one come and occupy it? Why is it that other denominations have teachers here and we have none, especially when the cause we plead flourishes so well wherever it is faithfully preached?''

E. G. Browning writes to *The Christian-Evangelist* from Myrtle Creek in 1855 as follows: ''The Umpqua Valley is divided into two counties, and there are some disciples in almost every neighborhood, with whom I have become acquainted, but no public preacher.''

The cry was answered. It was not long until a church of 7 members was organized at Looking Glass Prairie by a preacher named Chapman. Cole's Valley soon had the gospel message also. The Umpqua Valley is today a stronghold of Christians only, and the origin of its present day strength was back there in the early '50s with a mere handful of faithful disciples.

Another far cry came to Oregon brethren in 1855 from Washington Territory through Wm. Murphey, a resident of that territory. No response was given. The following year the appeal was renewed. Two brethren were selected to go, one of whom was James R. Fisher. They got as far as Portland, but, owing to Indian difficulties, they deemed it prudent to defer the trip. The appeal was renewed again the following year and Brother Fisher, accompanied by a Brother Casteel, determined to go to their assistance. The reports do not state whether this effort was successful or not; but they did reach Rainier, on the Oregon side of the Columbia River and found there ''a small church organized a little time before by Brother Huntington.'' Thus the gospel went out in eccentric circles, ever widening as the years passed by.

This period was a critical one. In the middle '50s J. R. Fisher wrote to *The Christian-Evangelist* from Pleasant Hill as follows: ''We object to such phraseology in religious journals as 'fair play,' 'hands off,' 'stand back,' etc. Such bullying language does not sound harmoniously upon the pages of a religious periodical that is visiting monthly thousands of Christian homes, and moulding them and their families as disciples of the Lord Jesus.''

There is no indication as to what publication is referred to, but we are inclined to respond, Amen. Nor is there a hint as to what the objection refers to.

An example of New Testament discipline is gleaned from this period. In *The Christian-Evangelist* of 1858 J. R. Fisher writes concerning the practice at the Pleasant Hill church: ''We consider it the duty of the elders to visit their flocks from house to house as well as to furnish religious instruction upon the first day of the week. In case of a public transgression, or waywardness, the elders labor with the offender; if suitable reparation is made by him it goes no further; if not, they proceed to collect the evidence in the case, giving the accused an opportunity to confront those who testify against him and to defend himself if he wishes to do so. After which the elders proceed to give a decision in the case; regarding not only the magnitude of the offence, but also the sufficiency of the evidence to sustain the accusation. Cases of difficulty among the brethren are treated the same way, after the preliminary steps have been taken as set forth in the 18th chapter of Matthew. All this is done without confusion, and without having a democratic mass meeting of the congregation. After they give their decision, they proceed to publicly report the same to the church. After which the members withdraw from the offender according to the command in 1 Cor. 5:11, 12. We avoid the investigation of cases of discipline by or in the presence of the mass of the church, as uncomely, sometimes indecent, un-Scriptural, and every way fraught with the worst consequences. We avoid voting by the church except upon questions of expediency. We look upon voting as tending more or less to factionism. All propositions that any member may wish to present to the church are first privately placed in the hands of the elders, which it is their duty to consider. If they think it will tend to the good of all then they lay it before the church, for adoption or rejection—Acts 21:18-26. We also apply this rule in case of application for letters."

This is good material for modern elders. Churches would be saved much grief if they were to follow this simple, plain, sensible procedure. There is perhaps no phase of church life and procedure that is so little understood as the matter of discipline. Some elders even think that "discipline" has no other meaning than to turn out of church. The word literally means teaching; when applied to a case of wrongdoing it bears the significance of turning in the right direction. Every sermon ought to be disciplinary; likewise the Bible School lesson and the Christian Endeavor prayer meetings; the effect of official board meetings and all business meetings should be disciplinary. When it is necessary to inflict punishment for wrongdoing there are other methods than withdrawing fellowship. When that becomes necessary it should be accomplished according to Scriptural methods, always keeping the eye single to the saving of the offender and the protection of the congregation from schism as a result. We would commend the above excerpt as worthy of consideration to every elder in our churches.

CHAPTER IV

ORGANIZATION

Men have been called "social animals." They group themselves around kindred ideas. Common duties, common problems, common pleasures, common roads produce a kinship among people. In a land, or under conditions where common bonds are limited, the social feature is accentuated all the more. The pioneer days of Oregon presented such conditions. Communities were small and there was practically but one occupation—farming, or something kindred. The whole population was forced very largely into the same groove of action. Their work, their play, their worship found common expression. Unified interests resulted in unified activities. Likewise, the social instinct followed the only outlet of expression possible—the church. Hence, the social gatherings of that day were the church gatherings.

This early period was a time of turmoil in the religious world. Denominationalism was at its best; sectarianism, at its worst. An article of faith could not be proclaimed without some one being ready to take up the gauntlet in opposition or defense. Sermons were not "moral essays," but "doctrinal treatises." The objective in preaching was not so much to induce "holy living," as it was to buttress the faith. The cause of primitive Christianity did not find a welcome among the denominations on the field. The opposition to "Christians only" is vividly portrayed by a news item from James McBride in 1854:

"People in Oregon are much more open to conviction, have fewer prejudices wherewith to bolt the door of the

47

heart against us, than I have witnessed in any other country. . . . . There is a portion of our sectarian neighbors who are 'not a whit behind' any in any place; and a stern and fiery opposition is unremittingly displayed by the clergy thereof.''

The effect of this opposition was to build up a defense that was well nigh impregnable. Many a doughty sectarian knight felt the cold steel of the Sword of the Spirit in the hand of a Christian only, and much to the knight's discomfiture. The average preacher of that day was not one step behind the old darky in the Southland, who, as he was coming up out of the baptismal water, looked proudly about him and said, ''Now I'se ready to 'spute!''

These conditions drove the pioneer disciples to cooperation, a cooperation which imperceptibly grew into organization. The cooperative life and activities of the disciples in Oregon naturally fall into four separate epochs. This chapter is intended only as a sketch, or outline of these epochs. Yet, the history of the first three is so meager that an outline is about all that can be given of it.

I.   1852-1860

In 1852 Glen O. Burnett called the disciples of the Valley to assemble together for fellowship and worship. This was hailed as an inspiration. This first meeting was held in an oak grove near the present town of McCoy. Perhaps none then realized the far reaching consequences of that first meeting; but it was the genesis of the missionary work of Disciples of Christ in Oregon which has broadened into an ever widening stream of gospel effort. It was also the first of the annual gatherings that have been faithfully perpetuated from that time to this.

Out of this first fellowship meeting at McCoy grew the "annual meeting." This was not a "convention." A convention would doubtless have been unorthodox at that time. It would have smacked of creeds and ecclesiasticism. On the contrary these meetings were merely preaching services—three sermons a day, nor were they sermonettes. The time between sermons was spent in social intercourse. Gradually they introduced the feature of hearing reports from the various churches represented. Then a little business was introduced, an evangelist was chosen, etc., until, before the congregations realized it, they were simply threads in one fabric, inextricably interwoven into each other.

In these beginning days a missionary work of modern type would have been utterly impossible, except from an outside source. That source was not available. The logical thing to do was to unify themselves and build up a group consciousness. The camp meeting bound the churches together as dependent parts. Unconsciously to them, God was developing these churches to the point where they not only would recognize the mutual dependency of churches upon each other, but also to the point where they would recognize the necessity of group solidarity if they would evangelize the territory. Through this the approach to organized missionary work later was easy.

These gatherings continued under the name of "annual meetings" until 1860. It is quite certain that there was no failure any year to meet, but the place is not always discoverable. From McCoy in 1852 it appears to have gone in 1853 to Rickreal, and in 1854 to Luckimute, all in Polk county. We can find no mention of the meeting in 1855 or 1856. In 1857 the time is definitely located as in

September, but the place is missing. In September, 1858 it was held at Mill Creek, near the present town of Aumsville. Monmouth claimed it in August 1859, and on September 7, 1860 it met in Eola. Eola was then a place of some pretensions and had aspirations to become the capitol of the state when it was admitted to the Union. The story is told that a vote was taken to settle the location of the capitol, Salem and Eola being the chief contenders for the place; and that, when the votes were counted, Salem had won by a majority of one. This story is not borne out by historical records and is probably a myth, yet it is not beyond the range of probability. Eola, as a community, still exists, but the town is gone. The old church building in which the above mentioned meeting was held was the last one of the old pioneer landmarks to be torn down. It stood unoccupied and in a decaying condition for many years and was razed only in 1924. The old pulpit desk, from which many a mighty gospel message was preached, now stands in the tabernacle at Turner, a monument of pioneer days.

It was during this period, and through this annual meeting, that Oregon disciples attempted to assume some responsibility in a definite way for carrying out the Great Commission. It has been mentioned in a former chapter that John Powell was the first missionary to go through the valley preaching the gospel. There is no record as to how he was constituted a missionary, nor from whom he received his commission to go on his missionary journeys. It is not a great stretch of the imagination to suppose that the first annual meeting at McCoy in 1852 was responsible. In all probability it was not an "official" call. Most certainly it did not carry any backing other than moral support.

The record of the second annual meeting in 1853 at
Rickreal definitely states that John Rigdon was "appointed" evangelist. There was no stipend that went with
the appointment, but it did carry the endorsement of the
churches. As such evangelist he preached from Jackson-
ville, in the extreme south part of the state, to Steilacoom,
in Washington Territory, on the north.

At the meeting at Mill Creek in 1858 John Powell was
again appointed evangelist, this time officially, and as such
he labored all through the valley. In his commission by
the Annual Meeting he was authorized "to set in order the
things wanting and to instruct the officers of the congregation how to demean themselves in the house of God." It
would take a brave man to do that today; but we have
already noted that there were giants in those days.

II.   1860-1877

The second epoch of organized work in Oregon begins
with the annual meeting at Eola in 1860. The story of
that meeting is best told by the official records, and by one
who participated in them:

"Messengers from most of the congregations of the Christian
Church in Oregon, met at Eola, in Polk county, on the 7th inst.
(September, 1860). In annual meeting . . . . . Brother Jas. R.
Fisher was elected President, and Brother Wm. Porter, Secretary.
. . . . The Christian Missionary Society of Oregon, the members
of the Society to be members of the Christian Church, and the
object of the society to build up the kingdom of Christ in Oregon
. . . . was organized during the progress of the meeting. . . . .
The place for holding the next annual meeting was fixed at the
Silver Creek meeting house in Marion county, and the time was
. . . . Thursday next before the third Sunday of September."—
Wm. Porter, Sublimity, Oregon, Sept., 1860.

Thus, these pioneer churches definitely accepted the
obligations of the gospel and prepared themselves accord-

ingly to discharge it. This organization lasted until 1877, during which time the annual gathering was held at the following places: At Silver Creek, on the Thursday before the third Lord's Day in September, 1861; at Bethany in 1862 (this is not positively so stated in the records, but there is the definite statement that the annual meeting was held at Bethany in the '60s and, from the coordination of events, the writer is convinced that it was in 1862); at Central, seven miles east of Albany, October 1-6, 1863; at McMinnville in June, 1864; at Bethel in June, 1865; 1866 and 1867 are impossible to locate; at Monmouth in 1868; at La Creole (Rickreal) from 1869 to 1873; at Dixie (we have been told that Dixie and Rickreal are the same place) from 1874 to 1876; and at Dallas in June, 1877.

The year 1863 is a bit puzzling to the historian. We find the records of three different annual meetings that year, viz., at Eola, over the second Lord's Day in June; at Central Church, October 1-6; and at Monmouth in December. There is a difference in designations by which these meetings were recorded. At Eola it was the "annual meeting"; at Central it was the "state convention"; and at Monmouth it was the "state cooperation." We are inclined to credit the meeting at Central as being in the true line of succession for two reasons: First, the length of the meeting—it was a whole week. The great length would denote an importance that did not attach to the other meetings. Second, the business that was transacted at the meeting at Central would indicate that it was the regular, official meeting of the churches. The state was divided into seven missionary districts at this meeting, as follows: 1. Douglas and Coos counties; 2. Lane and Benton counties; 3. Linn and Marion counties, and Lane north of the Willamette River; 4. Clackamas county and Multnomah county east of the Willamette River; 5. Polk, Yamhill and Washington counties; 6. Columbia, Clatsop and Tillamook counties, and Multnomah west of the Willamette River; 7. All the section east of the Cascade Mountains.

That meeting at Central also passed a resolution to establish a Christian College. A Committee was appointed as follows: Central Church, John H. Lines; Luckimute, Z. Davis; McMinnville, Wm. Dawson; Upper Muddy, C. C. Davis; Eola, H. M. Waller; Silver Creek, Thomas Wilbur (this is the way the name appears in the report. An historian who has specially studied the Silver Creek country declares it his belief that this was Fones Wilbur); Mill Creek, Wm. Porter; Scio, J. W. Richardson; Monmouth, H. Bufford; Salem, A. Stanton; Dallas, Wm. Menefee; Butte Creek, W. G. Maser (Mascher?); Salt Creek, Jas. G. Campbell; Antioch, Jas. P. Morgan; Harris Bridge, Samuel Bailey; Pleasant Hill, Wm. Bristow; Dallas, Curtis Whitson; Looking Glass Prairie, Brother Todd; Coast Fork, D. B. White; Cannonville (Canyonville?), S. B. Briggs. The committee agreed to meet on the first day of June, 1864. There is no record of that meeting. There is no record that any action was ever taken to establish a school in accordance with the resolution. It is presumed that this committee, like many another we are all familiar with, promptly forgot about it.

III.   1877-1888

The third period of organized work in Oregon began with the annual meeting at Dallas in 1877. At this meeting it was voted to discontinue the ''annual meetings, and in lieu thereof an annual cooperation meeting of delegates of the churches was instituted. . . . The business of the Cooperation was defined to be to receive reports of committees, gather statistics, provide for the vigorous prosecution of evangelical and missionary work, and such other purely executive matters, pertaining to the advancement of Christ's kingdom as may come before it.''

Previous to this meeting we can find no mention whatever that the churches shared the expenses of the evangelists in their arduous tasks. One of the steps in advance over the ''annual meeting'' which the ''Cooperation'' took was that the churches were ''to provide the means.'' That was a long step in advance. The second epoch of organized work had called itself a ''missionary convention''; but evidently it was in name only that it was missionary. By 1877 the brethren were getting in dead earnest. During the first year of the Cooperation thirty churches contributed $449.25 for the support of the work. Eight or ten evangelists were assisted during that year, and as a result we read that ''the churches were generally quickened and strengthened; stimulated largely by their own active benevolence, and the cooperative labors of the earnest and devoted evangelists.''

The second meeting of the Cooperation was held at Monmouth in November, 1878. The first year had been successful beyond their hopes. During the second year a reaction set in, and at the third meeting of the Cooperation in 1879, again held at Monmouth, there was consternation. Practically nothing had been contributed. The evangelists had again been upon their own resources. Facing the situation unfalteringly they reorganized the work and Peter R.

Burnett was commissioned to canvass the churches east
of the Willamette River, and Bruce Wolverton was given
the same task on the west side.

At that third meeting of the Cooperation it was decided
to center all their efforts for the coming year upon "the
one purpose of laying a proper foundation of building up
a Christian Church in the city of Portland." About $2,400
was subscribed for this cause from disciples outside of
Portland.

In 1880 the Cooperation met in Portland, November 9;
in 1881, at Amity, November 8-11; in 1882, at Eugene,
October 18-21; in 1883, at Salem, October 3-6; in 1884, at
Portland, in June; in 1885 the meeting was held at Turner
where it has been held continuously ever since with one
exception.

The early '80s are shrouded in obscurity. Except the
effort to aid the cause in Portland little is recorded except
the fact of the annual gatherings. Nor can we determine
the exact date of the closing of the State Cooperation and
the organization of the Christian Missionary Convention
of Oregon. The minutes of the meeting in Eugene in 1882,
and of the meeting in Salem in 1883, are still extant and
published together in a single booklet entitled, "Report
of the Christian Missionary Convention of Oregon." It
operated under a constitution, the first such document we
have record of among the churches. It is not unlikely
that somewhere in the '80s the name of the Cooperation
was changed to Christian Missionary Convention of
Oregon, and that in the reports sometimes one name is
used and sometimes the other.

IV. 1888-PRESENT TIME

When the Annual State Cooperation was organized at
Dallas in 1877 the camp meeting feature for the state
gatherings was discontinued and county gatherings began
to be organized upon the camp meeting plan. The county
meetings began to rival the state meetings in popularity
and attendance. In 1873 grove meetings began to be held
near Aumsville. They became so popular they could not
accommodate the people. In 1878 the place of the county
meeting was changed to Turner in order to better accommodate the crowds that came. A grove was prepared for
a Fourth of July celebration and was converted to the
use of this meeting. It was in the bend of the river on the
edge of the village of Turner, the ground belonging to the
Turner family. A small tabernacle was built and this became thence the home of the county meetings. On May
17, 1878 the Turners deeded to the Christian Association
of Marion County 6.19 acres of land to be used for the
annual meeting. The county meeting was finally merged
into the state meeting in 1885 and the property was afterwards deeded to the Christian Missionary Convention of
Oregon. The state society was incorporated under that
name on October 9, 1888. This is the landmark from which
we date the beginning of the fourth epoch of our organized
work. The incorporators were D. M. Doty, President;
Peter R. Burnett, Corresponding Secretary; H. C. Porter,
Secretary; J. W. Cowls, and H. A. Johnson. In 1891
George Turner and his sister, Mrs. Cornelia A. Davis,
erected the present tabernacle in memory of their father
and mother. A quit claim deed to the property was
executed giving the Convention full and free title to the
property forever. The tabernacle is a monumental build-

ing. The framework is constructed of heavy timbers, bolted together with wooden pins, the whole amply and substantially braced. It is seated at present for 1,500 people; but there is sufficient room for 500 more seats. An ample platform, with committee and office rooms, make it one of the finest convention halls in the state. It was a monumental gift, and one that would be rated in the present day at not less than $25,000.

Somehow in the course of years the legal name of the Convention suffered a rearrangement of the words in its title and it became known in actual usage as The Oregon Christian Missionary Convention. Practically, the change was insignificant, but courts sometimes stand on minute exactness. Many of our legal papers bore the popular title, and our corporation seal bore the same; but the incorporation papers bore the legal name. It was felt wise to make a correction, and as the least disturbing of all remedies it was decided to change the name of the corporation to agree with that in popular use. So, in 1912 supplementary Articles of Incorporation were filed changing the name from The Christian Missionary Convention of Oregon to THE OREGÓN CHRISTIAN MISSIONARY CONVENTION.

During the early days of this convention great crowds thronged annually to its meetings. The problem of caring for the teams was a vital one. It was decided to purchase an adjoining piece of land of about three acres and a contract therefor was made with the Turners. With the advent of the automobile the team problem became less and less until it was eliminated entirely. The indebtedness on the land purchased was piling up unpaid interest, and there was little concern on the part of the people to pay for the land. It seemed wise to dispose of this property which was done by selling it back to the Turners upon terms most reasonable to the Convention.

In 1911 the National Convention of Christian Churches was held in Portland during the middle of July. The date was closely following upon the regular time for the state convention. The State Board had the conviction that it would be difficult to obtain a large attendance at Turner so closely preceding the National Convention. So it was decided to coordinate the two by holding the state convention in Portland that year two days prior to the national gathering. This was done with excellent results.

CHAPTER V

THE OREGON CHRISTIAN MISSIONARY CONVENTION

In the previous chapter we have traced the evolution of our organized work in Oregon as follows:

I. 1852 to 1860. Annual gatherings of Oregon disciples commenced; organization only sufficient for the orderly conduct of these meetings; purely religio-social gatherings; missionary work not attempted beyond the endorsement of evangelists who went on their own charges.

II. 1860 to 1877. In 1860 the missionary obligation was definitely accepted by the organization of the Christian Missionary Convention of Oregon; little came of it beyond the development of sentiment, but it prepared the way.

III. 1877 to 1888. In 1877 the actual beginning of missionary work was made, and an attempt to further it by changing the organization to the Annual Christian Cooperation; county camp meetings began to appear, and the state gathering began to assume more and more the aspects of a convention, executive functions appearing.

IV. 1888 to the present time. In 1888 the work was incorporated under the laws of the state and a definite, progressive program was begun. This chapter attempts to deal with that effort.

NAME

One of the confusing matters in the early history is the evident confusion of names. In the beginning it was simply "The Annual Meeting." In 1860 the "Christian

59

Missionary Society of Oregon'' appears in regular form. During this time we meet with the names ''Annual Meeting,'' ''State Convention,'' and ''Cooperation.'' We take it that these were merely popular expressions, perhaps most largely for the sake of diversity, while the name assumed in 1860 was the parliamentary designation. In 1877, however, the name was actually changed to the ''Annual State Cooperation.'' It seems that the intention was to stimulate effort by a change in cognomen. The early fathers understood psychology. But the name was not popular. It would seem that it was never generally accepted.

As early as 1882 we find the printed records bearing the name of the ''Christian Missionary Convention of Oregon.'' This was only the substitution of the word ''convention'' for the older, and more usual, name of ''society.'' Just when this latter title was assumed we have no records to reveal. It was under this title that the work was first incorporated under the laws of the state. In the course of time it became in popular usage the ''Oregon Christian Missionary Convention.'' Practically it was the same name—just a different order of words. Just as ''Church of Christ'' and ''Christian Church'' have identically the same meaning, so these two names of the state work meant the same thing. But the law is sometimes very exacting even about the use and order of words. In a technical, legal sense the Christian Missionary Convention of Oregon was not the Oregon Christian Missionary Convention. It was not until 1912 that the discovery was made that many deeds to property were held by the ''Oregon Christian Missionary Convention,'' and the corporate seal bore that name, while the legal, incorporated name was the "Christian Missionary Convention of Oregon." The Corresponding Secretary took the matter up with the Attorney General of the State of Oregon, and upon his advice the Articles of Incorporation were so changed as to conform the name of the society to the popular usage. This was done by authority of the convention in 1912.

CONSTITUTION

There are three constitutions extant, all providing in a general way the same form of organization, differing only in minor details. A history should preserve the important documents of an institution; and, that these may be preserved for future generations, they are given here.

The First Constitution

The first constitution is found in the minutes of the meeting of 1882. The date of its adoption is not indicated. It is as follows:

ARTICLE I.—This Association shall be known as the Christian Missionary Convention of Oregon.

ARTICLE II.—It shall be composed, when in session, of the accredited delegates from the several congregations.

ARTICLE III.—Each congregation shall be entitled to be represented by two delegates, and if their number is fifty, by three; and one for each additional fifty or major portion.

ARTICLE IV.—At each annual meeting there shall be elected the following officers, who shall represent the Convention, when the same is not in session, to wit: A President, Vice President, Treasurer, Recording Secretary and Corresponding Secretary. These shall constitute an Executive Board for the transaction of all business of the Convention during the time intervening between meetings of the Convention, subject to the directions of the Convention. The Executive Board shall have the right, when so directed, to employ an evangelist or evangelists, to select fields of labor, and to direct and control the labors of said evangelist or evangelists.

ARTICLE V.—The Executive Board shall meet once a quarter, and at such other times as shall be indicated by the call of the President, and at all meetings three members shall be a quorum for the transaction of business.

ARTICLE VI.—The quarterly meetings shall be held on the first Tuesday in January, April, July and October, at such places as may be agreed upon.

ARTICLE VII.—The President shall preside at all meetings of the Executive Board, and at all meetings of the Convention when present. The Vice President shall preside in the absence of the President. The Recording Secretary shall keep all the records of the meetings of the Convention, and of the meetings of the Executive Board. The Corresponding Secretary shall be the correspondent both for the Executive Board and Convention. The Treasurer shall receive and pay out, upon the warrant of the Corresponding Secretary, attested by the President, all moneys contributed for missionary purposes.

ARTICLE VIII.—It shall also be the duty of the Executive Board to provide a programme for the annual meeting, to endeavor to keep the churches alive to the interests of missions, to notify all churches of the time set for taking collections for missions, and to furnish the churches with blank statistical reports two months in advance of the time of the annual meeting, to be used for reporting the condition of the churches.

ARTICLE IX.—It shall be the duty of churches engaged in this Convention to be represented, if possible, at all annual meetings by delegates; to take quarterly collections on the first Lord's Day in January, April, July and October, or on another Lord's Day near that time, when the day set is not convenient, and to forward said collection at once to the Treasurer.

ARTICLE X.—The following committees shall constitute the working force of the Convention, and shall consist of three members each:

1. On Credentials.

2. Time and Place of Next Meeting.

3. Auditing Committee.

4. On Resolutions.

5. On Constitution.

These shall be appointed at each annual meeting, and shall report to the Convention in writing, which report may be accepted, rejected, or amended. The first two shall continue until their work for that Convention is done. The other three shall be standing committees, and shall continue until next Convention, and until others shall be chosen.

ARTICLE XI.—The Convention shall hold annual sessions at such time and place as shall be agreed upon at last session.

ARTICLE XII.—This constitution may be revised or amended at any Convention upon recommendation of Committee on Constitution, by a two-thirds vote of the Convention.

The reader will note that this was a "delegate" convention. The controversy over delegate conventions had not yet struck the brotherhood. From bits of evidence here and there it seems that the delegate feature was strictly enforced in the beginning, but it gradually faded out until this constitutional provision became a dead letter. It was still a provision of the constitution up to 1928, but the author has never known of even the suggestion of enforcing it.

Perhaps the most striking feature of this constitution is the requirement (a "duty" constitutes a requirement) to take quarterly collections for state missions. The growth of our missionary work in all the world, and the consequent multiplicity of missionary objectives, would make such a practice impossible today. But with no other work being attempted by the churches it was a very wise requirement for that day. The records do not say how many churches obeyed the constitution.

The Second Constitution

The second constitution was adopted in 1888, at the time of the incorporation of the Convention. It pretends to be an original document. But a comparison with the first shows how difficult it is to get away from stereotyped forms and conventions. It follows:

ARTICLE I.—This organization shall be called the Oregon Christian Missionary Convention.

ARTICLE II.—Its object shall be to devise ways and means for the spread of the gospel and the establishment of Churches of Christ in the State of Oregon, and to cooperate with the General Christian Missionary Convention.

ARTICLE III.—This Convention shall be composed of the officers of the Convention, of delegates from the churches of Oregon, of annual and life members, and such other brethren as the Convention may seat by majority vote.

2. Every Church of Christ in Oregon shall be entitled to two delegates for its organization and one additional delegate for every fifty members or major fraction thereof.

3. Any member of the Church of Christ in Oregon, providing his standing is good in some local organization, may become an annual member of this Convention by paying into its treasury the sum of two dollars, or he may become a life member by paying into its treasury the sum of twenty-five dollars, in five annual installments of five dollars each.

ARTICLE IV.—The officers of this Convention shall be a President, a Vice President, a Recording Secretary, a Corresponding Secretary, and a Treasurer, all of whom shall be elected at the annual meeting of this Convention and shall hold office until their successors are chosen.

2. The officers of this Convention shall constitute a State Board, and the majority members of said State Board shall constitute a quorum for the transaction of all business when the Convention is not in session.

3. It shall be the duty of the Corresponding Secretary to solicit funds, gather statistics and general information concerning the churches, and perform such other labor of the Convention as the State Board may appoint. His compensation shall be fixed by the State Board, and he shall make annual report in writing to this Convention.

4. Other officers of this Convention shall perform the duties which usually and naturally devolve upon said officers.

ARTICLE V.—The Convention shall meet annually at Turner, Oregon, upon such date as may be annually set by the Convention, or date fixed upon by the Official Board, should the Convention at any time see fit to leave it to their judgment.

ARTICLE VI.—All obligations and liabilities of this Convention under the former basis of Cooperation are continued under this constitution.

ARTICLE VII.—This constitution cannot be changed or amended unless such change or amendment is submitted in writing to the Executive Board at least three months before the annual meeting of the Convention. Said Board must cause to be published such proposed change or amendment in the religious papers of the Brotherhood on the coast, and said change or amendment must receive two-thirds of all votes present at the Convention.

The Third Constitution

The third constitution makes no pretense of originality, but is the second one amended. We give it here as it stood upon the records of the Convention until July 3, 1928 when it was still further amended.

ARTICLE I.—This organization shall be called the Oregon Christian Missionary Convention.

ARTICLE II.—Its object shall be to devise ways and means for the spread of the gospel and the establishment of churches of Christ in the State of Oregon, and to cooperate with General Christian Missionary Convention.

ARTICLE III.—This Convention shall be composed of the officers of the Convention, of delegates from the various churches of Oregon, annual and life members, and such other brethren as the Convention may seat by a majority vote.

2. Every Church of Christ in Oregon shall be entitled to two delegates for its organization, and one additional delegate for every fifty members or major part thereof.

3. Any member of the Church of Christ in Oregon, providing his standing is good in some local organization, may become an annual member of this Convention by paying into its treasury the sum of $2.00, or he may become a life member by paying into its treasury the sum of $25.00 in five annual installments of $5.00 each.

ARTICLE IV.—The officers of the Convention shall be a President, one Vice President for each district into which the state may be divided, not to exceed six in all, a Recording Secretary, a Corresponding Secretary, a Treasurer, a State Bible School Superintendent, and a State Christian Endeavor Superintendent.

2. The President, Vice Presidents, Recording Secretary, and Treasurer, shall be elected at the annual meeting of this Convention, and shall hold their offices until their successors are elected and qualified. The Corresponding Secretary shall be elected by the

Convention, and his term of office shall be indefinite, to cease upon ninety days notice in writing to be given by either party to the other. The State Bible School Superintendent shall be elected annually by the State Bible School Session of the Convention. The State Christian Endeavor Superintendent shall be elected annually by the State Christian Endeavor Session of the Convention.

3. The aforesaid officers of this Convention shall constitute a State Board, which shall have power to transact business when the Convention is not in session. Five members shall constitute a quorum. The State Board shall make all appropriations for missionary work and shall employ all missionaries. It shall have power to vacate the office of Corresponding Secretary during the fiscal year; and shall have power to fill all vacancies that may occur on the State Board, such appointees to serve until the next annual meeting of the Convention, or until their successors are elected and qualified.

4. It shall be the duty of the Corresponding Secretary to solicit funds, gather statistics and general information concerning the churches, and such other labor as the State Board may appoint. His compensation shall be fixed by the Board, and he shall make annual reports in writing to the Convention.

5. A chairman of the Convention shall be elected at the beginning of the annual sessions of the O. C. M. C., whose duty it shall be to preside over the annual session, appoint the committees thereof, and such other duties as naturally belong to a presiding officer.

6. The other officers of this Convention shall perform the duties which usually devolve upon said officers, and in addition to the above named duties the several Vice Presidents shall act as Superintendents of Missions in the districts from which they are respectively chosen.

ARTICLE V. This Convention shall meet annually at Turner, Oregon, upon such date as may annually be set by the Convention, or date fixed upon by the Official Board should the Convention see fit at any time to leave it to their judgment.

ARTICLE VI. All obligations and liabilities of this Convention under the former basis of cooperation are continued under this constitution.

ARTICLE VII. This constitution cannot be changed or amended unless such change or amendment is submitted in writing to the Executive Board at least three months before the annual meeting of the Convention. Said Board must cause to be published such proposed change or amendment in the religious papers of the Brotherhood on the coast. Said change or amendment must receive two-thirds of all the votes present at the Convention.

The change in the term of office of the Corresponding Secretary, and giving the State Board power to vacate his office and fill vacancies ad interim, was made at the convention of 1911.

The addition of the State Bible School Superintendent to the State Board was made July 31, 1917.

The addition of the State Christian Endeavor Superintendent to the State Board was July 3, 1923.

In the course of years some merited criticisms upon this constitution grew up, prominent among which were the following:

1. The matter of "buying" membership in the convention has fallen into discard with growing tendency to raise missionary money by the church itself instead of direct from the individual.

2. The matter of a "delegate" convention is strictly a dead letter.

3. The existence of two secretaries has been confusing and makes necessary exceedingly long titles.

4. The manner of fixing the date of the annual convention is an impractical one in these days.

5. Article VI is dead in consequence of those obligations contemplated thereunder having been fully discharged many years ago.

6. The constitution does not positively provide for its amendment. The Article dealing with that point needs a rewriting.

In view of these defects in the constitution the State Board prepared amendments to be offered to the 1928 convention for the virtual revision of the whole. That revision is as follows:

ARTICLE I. The name of this organization shall be THE OREGON CHRISTIAN MISSIONARY CONVENTION.

ARTICLE II. Its object shall be to devise ways and means for the spread of the gospel, and the establishment of churches of Christ, in the State of Oregon.

ARTICLE III. This Convention shall be composed of members of churches of Christ in the State of Oregon who shall assemble in the regular meetings thereof for the purpose of promoting its objects as stated in ARTICLE II. Any member of the Church of Christ in Oregon may become a Life Member of this Convention by paying into its treasury the sum of $25.00.

ARTICLE IV. The officers of this Convention shall be a President, one Vice President for each district into which the state may be divided, a Recorder, a Secretary, a Treasurer, a State Bible School Superintendent, and a State Christian Endeavor Superintendent.

2. The President, Vice Presidents, Recorder and Treasurer shall be elected at the annual meeting of this Convention, for a period of one year, or until their successors shall have been elected and qualified. The Secretary shall be elected by the Convention, for an indefinite period, his tenure of office to cease upon ninety days notice to be given in writing by either party to the other. The State Bible School Superintendent shall be elected annually by the State Bible School Session of the Convention. The State Christian Endeavor Superintendent shall be elected annually by the State Christian Endeavor Session of the Convention.

3. The aforesaid officers of this Convention shall constitute a State Board which shall have power to transact all business when the Convention is not in session. Five members shall constitute a quorum. The State Board shall make all appropriations and shall employ all missionaries. It shall have the power to vacate the office of Secretary during the fiscal year; and shall have power to fill all vacancies that may occur on the State Board, such appointees to serve until the next annual meeting of the Convention, or until their successors are elected and qualified.

4. It shall be the duty of the Secretary to superintend the missionary work authorized by the State Board, to solicit funds therefor, to gather statistics, and such other labor as the State Board may appoint. His compensation shall be fixed by the State Board, and he shall make annual reports in writing to the Convention.

5. A chairman of the Convention shall be elected at the beginning of the annual sessions of the Oregon Christian Missionary Convention, whose duty it shall be to preside over the annual session, appoint the committees therefor, and such other duties as naturally belong to a presiding officer.

6. The other officers of this Convention shall perform the duties which usually devolve upon said officers, and in addition to the above named duties the several Vice Presidents shall act as superintendents of missions in the districts from which they are respectively chosen.

ARTICLE V. This Convention shall meet annually at Turner, Oregon, upon such date as may be set by the State Board.

ARTICLE VI. This Constitution may be amended at any annual meeting of the Convention, provided, that notice of such proposed amendment shall be given to the churches at least three months prior to such change; and provided further, that such amendment shall receive two-thirds majority of all votes cast.

This revision was adopted on July 3, 1928, and provides the constitution now in effect.

CONVENTIONS

Disciples of Christ have always been a convention loving people. The heart of our organized activities lies in this trait of character. It was in them that organized effort was born, and largely through them is organized work perpetuated. Lacking an ecclesiasticism to bind the various churches together into a working body the conventions have furnished the spirit that has kept the body alive and active. Many of these conventions, or annual meetings, were largely local in character; and it is difficult, even impossible, to determine from the meager records always just what were local and what deserved the dignity of being denominated "state" conventions. It was a county gathering purely that paved the way for the present meeting place at Turner for the annual convention.

The time for these conventions was variously set from June to December. Crop conditions and weather gradually located the annual convention in the month of June; and, from 1884 to 1914, with only one exception, the records show June to be the time preferred. That one exception

was in 1911, and the change was made to July that year
on account of the National Convention being held in Portland in that month. The State Board felt that many people would be prevented from attending either the State
Convention or the National Convention if they were held
near together in time but apart in place. The fear was,
too, that the preference would not be given to the State
Convention. So, after full consideration, and with the
desire to help both conventions to the utmost, it was decided to call the State Convention to meet in Portland that
year immediately prior to the National Convention, and
abbreviate the sessions to the utmost, thus giving every
convention lover the opportunity of attending both conventions on one trip. The change was justified by the
results.

By 1914, conditions that had hitherto made June the
preferable month for the convention had quite materially
changed; the convention was regularly experiencing a
soaking rain during its sessions. It was observed that to
move the time up into the first of July it would avoid very
much of the discomfort of the rains and would meet the
convenience of the masses as regards crop demands quite
as well. The move was made, and with one single exception, has been adhered to. That exception was experi-
mental, hoping to attract a larger number of people.
Accordingly in 1917 the date was moved up to the first
part of August, but the experiment did not produce the
desired result and it was moved back to the first of July
where it has since remained. No doubt in the course of
time other conditions will arise that may make another
change necessary. But that remains for future generations and this is a history, not a prophecy.

SECRETARIES

The work of the State Board has always centered very largely around the State Secretary, commonly called the Corresponding Secretary. He is the one salaried agent of the State work and upon him necessarily devolves the executive work of the society. Prior to 1877 there is very little record of the official personnel of the organization. In 1860 Wm. Porter, of Sublimity, was the Secretary. Reuben Doty held that honor in 1863. From that time until 1877 we can find no trace of Secretaries. Up to this time the work of the State Secretary was principally clerical, that of recording minutes and corresponding with the churches.

In 1877 Bruce Wolverton was elected Secretary. He afterwards became the first pastor of the First Church in Portland. The next year S. C. Adams was elected and remained in that position for four years, when Bruce Wolverton was again elected. In 1883 J. W. Spriggs was elected. This is the only mention in the records we can find of this man. From that time on until 1888 there is no record of the incumbent of the Secretary's office. In 1888 Peter R. Burnett was elected and served two years. In 1890 J. F. Stewart was elected and served two years. It was the writer's pleasure to meet this good man in California in the summer of 1926, well advanced in years, but his memory had not grown dim concerning, nor had he ceased to love, Oregon. B. F. Mulkey succeeded Stewart and served two years lacking four months. L. F. Stephens filled out those four months of the second year. Mr. Mulkey afterwards strayed from the ministerial path to serve as legislator, college president, district attorney, and is now a highly influential attorney in the city of Portland.

In 1894 J. B. Lister was elected and served for ten successive years. It was during this decade of history that Oregon Missions was launched into its fullest stride. Lister went everywhere through the state preaching the Word, organizing new churches, reviving dead ones, and strengthening weak ones. To this day we find his footprints as fresh as though they had been made yesterday. It was a pioneer work then and he did it in a pioneer way, the work of both Evangelist and Secretary. After resigning the Secretaryship in Oregon Brother Lister entered the field again in Northern Idaho, after which he settled in business at Hood River for a time. After an illness of several months he died at the home of his daughter, Mrs. J. R. Edwards, at Newport, Oregon, on March 23, 1927.

In 1904 J. J. Evans was called from Palo Alto, California, to the Secretaryship in Oregon. He served one year and resigned to enter the more congenial work of the pastorate. F. E. Billington, for several years pastor at Cottage Grove, was called to succeed him in 1905. He continued for three years and accomplished a great work, putting the Board on a financial basis such as had never before been known. Both Evans and Billington followed the policy of former years in combining the evangelistic with the clerical work. In the last year of Billington's service the State Board relieved the Secretary from the evangelistic work and made him responsible only for the executive side of the office. A separate evangelist was put in the field who was to give his whole time to holding meetings. With the growth of the work the executive labors have proved quite sufficient for one man to accomplish efficiently.

At the convention in 1908 C. F. Swander was called from his pastorate at McMinnville to the Secretaryship. With this year of writing (1928) he rounds out a full 20 years in the position. At the present time he is the oldest state secretary in point of service in the Brotherhood; and only one other has ever served longer in the state secretary's position than he.

The secretarial position has been an evolution from primitive conditions to the more complex ones of modern times. Originally he was the one man who did it all. The correspondence of the society was small and required but little time. Upon his shoulders was put the responsibility of holding meetings, and the correspondence was conducted from the seat of meetings. The work had a different capitol every time he moved to a new meeting place. The correspondence then consisted chiefly of reminders to the churches concerning the offerings. As the work grew, the number of churches increased, and the Secretary's work became more varied. He was called upon for counsel when churches got in deep waters. He was asked to assist churches to locate preachers, and to assist preachers in locating churches. Church fusses began to look to him for assistance in settlement. It was discovered that more missionary money could be raised by the Secretary's appeal than by the pastor's. So the offerings devolved upon him. The knowledge that he could raise missionary money gave churches the idea that he ought to be pretty good at raising money for other purposes. Consequently, when they had local debts they must raise they began to send for the Secretary as the man who could wave the magic wand and get money out of the other fellow. As missionary offerings began to increase the State Board began to support weak churches in addition to evangelists; that necessitated a superintendency which naturally fell upon the state secretary. The preparations for the annual conventions were his work also; as they grew in numbers and importance his work increased in that regard. Today he has his time filled with "the care of all the churches."

THE STATE BOARD

There has been little change in the method of constituting the State Board throughout the years. During all the years it has been made as representative as possible of the various sections of the state. At the present time the State Board is made up of eleven persons, a President, five Vice Presidents, a Recorder, a Secretary, a Treasurer, a State Bible School Superintendent, and a State Christian Endeavor Superintendent. The Board meets approximately once each quarter for the transaction of business. It has full power over all matters between conventions, but it has been very sparing about the exercise of this prerogative. The headquarters of the State Board was formerly wherever the State Secretary lived, but a definite location was chosen at Portland by the convention in 1908. The work grew finally to an extent where the Secretary's home could no longer accommodate it and in 1919 a down town office was opened.

PRESIDENTS

There is scant record of the Presidents of the Convention. It is not beyond the bounds of good judgment to suppose that Glen O. Burnett was chosen as the first one in the long series at that first meeting at McCoy in 1852. Jas. R. Fisher is the first one recorded as having received

that honor. He was elected in 1860. John E. Murphey
was selected in 1863. On November 4, 1879 Bruce Wolverton came to the chair, but he resigned before the close of
the year and Peter R. Burnett succeeded him. At the
meeting in November next J. W. Cowls was chosen. In
1882 Wm. H. Adams was elected and served two years.
Somewhere between 1884 and 1888 W. R. Williams was
placed in the chair, but for how long a time we cannot
determine. In 1888 D. M. Doty was elected. David Wetzel
was elected in 1891 and was succeeded in 1892 by C. A.
Sehlbrede, a prominent layman, afterwards Federal Judge
in Alaska. He served two years as President. W. H.
Hawley then served one year, W. H. Osborne two years,
and K. H. Sickafoose one year. At the convention in 1898
Morton L. Rose, pastor of the Eugene church, was chosen
and served two years. J. S. McCallum, also pastor of the
church at Eugene, followed him for one year. J. W. Jenkins, then our outstanding leader in Eastern Oregon, was
elected for two successive years. Following him Davis
Errett, pastor of the First Church at Salem served for
four consecutive years, and Albyn Esson then served for
six years. In 1917 F. T. Porter, pastor of the Salem
Church, was chosen and served until his enlistment for
overseas service in 1919. A. L. Crim, pastor of the Eugene
Church, filled out his unexpired term. At the convention
in 1919 E. V. Stivers, also pastor at Eugene, was chosen
and remains at the head of the Oregon work until this day
(1928).

In former years it was the custom for the President to
preside over the sessions of the annual conventions. Some
criticism arose in the course of time in which the State
Board was charged with being a self perpetuating body

in that the President would always appoint a Nominating Committee which would renominate the Board. The State Board pleaded "Not Guilty!" to the accusation by introducing an amendment to the constitution providing for the election of a separate presiding officer for all sessions of the Oregon Christian Missionary Convention at the annual meeting. This was done in 1912. History does not record whether or not the change has brought the desired result. The State Board manifested its good faith, however. As long as human nature remains in humanity even a little unregenerate some folks will criticise and will look with suspicion upon the efforts of even honest folk.

CHAPTER VI

ITEMS OF INTEREST

The real work of state missions by Disciples of Christ in Oregon began in 1877. It took a full quarter of a century to prepare themselves for active service. Doubtless there were many aching hearts because things went so slowly. Doubtless some became impatient and "kicked over the traces" because things didn't move more rapidly in a missionary way. Doubtless, too, there were some who held a tight rein on progress—some because of fearful hearts, some because of an anti-missionary sentiment, and some, perhaps, through motives of covetousness. But, whatever the cause, they were no different from people today, and for every temperament then we have a parallel even now. Yet those twenty-five years were not lost. They were a seed sowing time, a period of foundation building. In that time, just as truly as in apostolic times, did "all things work together for good to them that love the Lord"; and we, of the present day, can look back with a better perspective and see how true it was.

The annual meeting in 1877 was held at Dallas and "a series of resolutions were adopted, by which the annual meetings of the Christian brotherhood were discontinued, and in lieu thereof an annual cooperation meeting of delegates of the churches was instituted. . . . The business of the Annual Cooperation was defined to be, to receive reports of committees, gather statistics, provide for the vigorous prosecution of evangelical and missionary work,

77

and such other purely executive matters pertaining to the advancement of the interest of Christ's kingdom as may come before it.''

The thirty churches in the Cooperation provided the sum of $449.25 for the work of the ensuing year—quite a respectable amount for that day and number of churches. The second meeting of the Cooperation was held at Monmouth in November, 1878, and extensive plans for the ensuing year were made. They were intoxicated with the success of that first year's effort, and seemed not to realize that it might not continue forever. Their dream, however, was sadly shattered, for we read: ''The interest and zeal of the Cooperation and churches during the preceding year, in providing the means for energetic and general missionary work, seemed to be succeeded by a corresponding paralysis, so that the Board was unable to report any gratifying or satisfactory results at the third meeting of the Cooperation, held at Monmouth, November 4, 1879.''

But failure did not daunt those pioneers. The State Board met at Salem on December 5th following, and ''after mature and prayerful deliberation it was ordered that the missionary work throughout the state be prosecuted with all possible vigor.'' To carry out this mandate Peter R. Burnett was appointed to canvass Linn county, and the southern part of Marion county, for funds; and Bruce Wolverton was appointed to do the same work on the West side of the Willamette river.

At the meeting of the Cooperation in 1879 a specific missionary project was undertaken, that ''of laying a proper foundation of building up a Christian Church in the city of Portland.'' This church had been organized in February preceding and it had no certain dwelling place.

This effort of the Missionary Society was to provide a lot for a house of worship. Bruce Wolverton was commissioned particularly to accomplish this task. At the next meeting of the Cooperation, held in Portland on November 9, 1880, he reported that about $3,000 had been subscribed.

The general policy of missionary work, as adopted by those early pioneers, has been in vogue through all the years since. Among the resolutions passed at the state convention held in Eugene in 1882 is one that clearly defines this policy:

"That one of the principal, and first, works of the evangelist, or evangelists, shall be to labor among weak or broken down churches, with a view to having them engage in regular preaching; in this way, by having each church engage a preacher when able, and when one church is not able, to combine two or more in the employment of pastoral labor. In other words, to make an effort to bring together churches and preachers as indicated above; and, when an effort is made to plant churches, important towns and centers shall have the preference."

No one can question the wisdom of this policy when wisely directed. It is to the credit of that early day that it was adopted.

The convention of 1883 met at Salem, on October 3-6, and employed Neil Cheetham as evangelist for six months at a salary of $500 for the time. The resolutions recommended that the work be largely centered upon one place, but not to the entire exclusion of others. Albany was chosen as the field, and J. F. Floyd was sent to care for the work. The report of the Board for this year was very encouraging, noting particularly the growth of the church in Portland, the organization of a church at Forest Grove, the purchase of lots at Corvallis, and the faithfulness of the "few noble souls" at St. Helens. The report closes with the pathetic plea to "remember that in the two years there has been expended the sum of $337.45 for all purposes." That means that the evangelist did not get nearly all the salary promised him, and that the other work was carried on at the personal sacrifice of the missionaries. It is ever thus!

The period from 1883 to 1891 is one of silence so far as the record is concerned. Yet we are sure the work did not lapse. In 1891 the Convention met at Turner where there had been an annual meeting since 1885. The report of the Corresponding Secretary for that year bears some painfully familiar statements:

"In gathering the statistics some of our best churches, and some preachers, paid no attention to our letters asking them to fill out and return the blank reports sent them. Why this was I will not attempt to say; but will leave them to account for on the day of final reckoning."

The same difficulty is experienced even in this present day. Report blanks are sent to every church in the state, to some of them twice, and to some even the third and fourth time. Even then there are some who refuse to make report. Like the Secretary of bygone days the present incumbent harbors the vengeful hope that one of the questions asked of preachers and church officials by St. Peter on that day of final accounting will be, "Did you always faithfully fill out and return the annual statistical report blank?" We are willing, too, that mercy shall be extended to those who did not, for in no other way can some enjoy the blessings of eternity. The record continues:

"At the beginning of the fiscal year we asked the churches to loan their pastors to the Board for a short meeting. All seemed willing to do so, but for some reason only one or two responded."

That, too, is as fresh as if it had been written yesterday. Leaders everywhere are familiar with the steeds that are spirited in the pasture, but balky in the traces. The record continues:

"I have written 788 letters. Some have answered but many paid no attention to them."

That was a large number of letters to write in those days, for those were the days of longhand writing. Typewriters were not then in common use. Human nature has not changed materially since that early date. People expect a prompt reply if they write to a Secretary; and, if he fails entirely, he ought to be kicked out of the job! But when he writes to them—, O well! that's a different matter!

The report for the year shows that churches were organized at Lebanon and Newport, and Prineville was reorganized. Both Lebanon and Newport ceased as churches after this and were again reorganized, while Prineville has continued more or less regularly since that date. A Chinese Mission with 50 members was organized in Portland, and a Swedish Mission, conducted by A. Erickson, was reported in progress in Portland. Building activities amounting to $13,284.37 were in progress, and $87.50 was reported for Foreign Missions. This seems pitifully small to us in this present day, but when we remember that the cause of Foreign Missions among us was only eight years old at that time it is not an occasion for criticism. A total of $280.43 was expended for state work that year.

This convention went on record concerning two important world affairs, viz., the closing of the gates at the

World's Fair in Chicago on Sundays, and the drink traffic on the Congo. They are as follows:

"To the Commissioners of the Columbia Exposition, Chicago, Illinois:

"Your memorialists, the Disciples of Christ in Oregon, in convention assembled, believing that the interests of society, of morality and religion, as well as the interests of the Exposition itself, demand that the Exposition be closed on Sunday, do most respectfully ask that you adopt a rule closing the doors of the Exposition on Sunday."

The second resolution was presented by David Wetzle who was appointed a Committee to forward the same.

"WHEREAS, From Alaska to Madagascar, from Siberia to New Zealand, the nations groan under the terrible drink curse and the spectacle of their degradation and destruction is set before us in earnest appeals from missionaries, converted natives and even many of the officials, and

"WHEREAS, The Congo drink traffic is the most serious obstruction to the introduction of civilization and Christianity into that country, and believing that the action proposed by the Council of Brussels,—already concurred in by all European governments—will have a powerful influence in suppressing the giant evil, notwithstanding that the ratification of this treaty by OUR government is alone necessary to make it operative, therefore

"RESOLVED, That we view with astonishment and sincere regret the action of our government and do hereby appeal to the representatives of the people in our National Congress and urge upon them the duty of making the United States a party to the Brussels treaty.

"RESOLVED, That a copy of this action be sent to each of our United States senators with the request that they bring the subject before the body of which they are a member, use their personal influence and power toward securing a favorable action.

"RESOLVED, That a copy of this resolution be sent to the *Oregonian* for publication."

Those memorialists did not understand it then, but this last resolution was in the nature of a preparation for the great work afterwards undertaken by Disciples of Christ on the Congo and in which Oregon has played such a conspicuous part.

The pioneer field is particularly afflicted with the unworthy preacher problem. Pioneer Oregon was no exception. To such an extent was this true that the convention of 1893 passed strong resolutions which are well worth repeating for the present generation.

"We would lift up the standard of the ministry and plead for pure-hearted and clean-handed men for all of our pulpits. We deplore the fact that the churches in our state have been afflicted by impure and unworthy men, and that the cause of Christ has thus been greatly retarded. We declare that any man who is a vender, or user, of intoxicants, or who is unlawfully divorced or married, as measured by the law of Christ and not by the law of the state, or one who is known to be impure in his social relationships, is unworthy to be a minister and should not be recognized as such by the church of Christ.

"We urge upon our churches the importance of great care and rigid examination before allowing any man to occupy their pulpits.

"We would recommend (1), That the State Board keep a record of all our preachers of the state; that record to show the moral standing, whether good or bad, of each preacher in the state. (2), That any preacher coming to our state from another s..., be requested to present satisfactory evidence of his moral w... to the State Board; and further, that any preacher not kno... a congregation be not allowed to preach for them until... they ascertain his standing from the State Board, notwithstanding he may possess a pocketful of testimonials.

"We most cordially invite to our state all who are pure and worthy, and will extend to them a hearty welcome, but declare that we have no room for the lazy and immoral."

Amen! Succeeding generations have not been able, and will not be able, to improve upon that declaration. If a man is clean and worthy he will not fear the most rigid investigation. An objection to investigation is an invitation to the suspicion that it is needful. Pocket testimonials are worthless. Many of them are worthy of acceptance at their face value, yet they are unreliable. An unworthy man will not carry a testimonial that is not favorable: the giver of a letter will not give an unfavorable word to be carried in the pocket by the recipient; they may tell the truth as far as they go, but what they do not say would sometimes be most eloquent if the reader only knew. Some churches have a pernicious habit of giving an unworthy man a recommendation because they want to get rid of him. As a reader of "pocket" testimonials for many years the author must confess to a bit of suspicion every time one is pulled on him. The testimonial should be sent direct from the writer to the reader. Only in that way can it be accepted without suspicion.

Strenuous methods have sometimes been used to bring churches and preachers into cooperation. In the report of the 1900 convention we find a list of 58 churches that failed to make the annual report. The membership of each is listed. Four out of the 58 made a state offering tota... ...00 In a note attached to the list we find the ... ...ntence: "After the manner of men in peanu... ...ies it (the offering) could have been $2,578.00 a... ... supported 8 evangelists full time." The missionary... ...l is sore tried sometimes; likewise the missionary secret... 's soul. But the ones who went through those tryi...g times of the early days, and suffered the disappoint...ments incident thereto, may rest in the full assurance tha...t they did better than they knew; they laid a foundatio...n for the larger liberality of the present day. And we...may indulge the consolation that we, too, are paving the...way for a larger liberality tomorrow. We are reaping th...e fruitage now of seed sown then; tomorrow some one else...will be reaping the fruitage of the seed we are sowing toda...y. It is ever thus!

Notwithstanding such...discouragements there creep into the records from time to...time the most encouraging items. In the report for 1901 th...ere appears on the inside page of

the cover sheet, at the close of all these reports, in large
type, this heartening word:

"Our Missionary Organization, the O. C. M. C., has
made a rapid growth in its work the last five years. Then
we were $461.50 in debt. There was no missionary in the
state. Now we are out of debt and aiding in ten fields,
besides general evangelizing."

The grim monster of debt is always ready to strike his
fangs into the vitals of missionary work. It will happen
in the best regulated societies. At the convention in 1906
an indebtedness of $1836.86, not satisfactorily provided
for, was reported to the convention. A part of this was
for improvements on the grounds, and a part was for
back salaries to missionaries. This debt was entirely discharged during the three years' service of F. E. Billington
as Secretary. It has been the policy of the State Board
now for many years to conduct its work on a practically
cash basis. Sometimes it has been necessary to borrow
money for short periods, but an indebtedness has not been
allowed to accumulate. It is the only safe way to conduct
a missionary work. A missionary society must live within
its income just the same as the families from whom it
draws its support.

Oregon has always been foremost in good deeds. Her
missionary sympathies have not all been local. It was at
this convention of 1906 that announcement was made that
$2,000 was available for founding a Home for Orphans
and Aged in Oregon. A committee consisting of Albyn
Esson, E. C. Sanderson, Victor Dorris, G. S. O. Humbert,
and J. W. Jenkins was appointed to further the proposi-
tion. This move could not well be conducted under the
auspices of the State Board, so the state convention acted

merely as a clearing house to get a competent body to act upon it. The outgrowth of the matter was the establishment of the Home for the Aged in Eugene. This institution was afterwards moved to Walla Walla, Washington, and was taken over by the National Benevolent Association as a part of its great work.

Sometime during the early days of the convention at Turner a two story building was erected as sleeping quarters for delegates. It did not become increasingly popular as the years rolled on. It was familiarly known as the "Ark." Just what may have suggested that name we leave to the imagination of the reader. At the convention of 1910 it was decided to tear it down and construct another building for the same purpose. The work was put in charge of L. F. Stephens. Labor was donated and, before the summer was over, a new building was erected that has never failed to be filled to the limit at each convention. This building is known as the "Lodge."

Mention is made in a previous chapter of the purchase of a few acres of shaded ground just west of the tabernacle. About eight and one-third acres were included in this parcel. At the time of purchase the purpose was to get additional shade for the teams that came in such numbers on Sundays. The original purchase price was $1,000. Only a little had been paid on the purchase price by 1912, and there was considerable unpaid interest. With the advent of the automobile the presence of teams at the convention gradually diminished. It was getting more difficult all the time to arouse enthusiasm for raising the money for this debt. Sentiment for disposing of that parcel as unnecessary was growing. At the convention of 1910 an effort was made to raise it, but it ended in failure. By 1912 it was definitely decided to sell the property. Mr. Louis Turner, who held the note, very generously agreed to take back the property, surrender the note, and pay back to the Convention the amount of principal and interest that had been paid less the amount that would have been rental on the property for the time possessed at a very nominal rate. Upon that basis he paid about $115.00 to the Convention and took back the property. Further lapse of time fully vindicated the wisdom of this sale.

The convention of 1912 was "electrified" in reality by the presentation from the people of Turner of equipment for lighting the buildings and grounds with electricity. Before that time the only light available was coal oil lamps, which at best were dim and sputtering. Sputtering from the platform may be expected and tolerated; but from lights, never. The building is too large to be lighted in a really first class manner except with very high powered candles. But these lights were an improvement of which all were proud. Mr. R. D. Gray, the local banker, was very largely instrumental in the gift of this lighting system. At the convention of 1927 the lights were further improved.

A new departure in conventions was offered in 1916 with the institution of a convention for East Oregon. The thought in this was not in any way to supplant the Turner Convention, but to supplement it by giving East Oregon folks who could not go to Turner an opportunity to have a state convention come to them. Accordingly the experiment was tried at Pendleton, June 21-25, 1916. There were 123 registrations from outside the city of Pendleton at that first convention. The experiment proved so pleasing that it was decided to continue it as an annual affair. They have been held as follows: Pendleton, 1916; La Grande, 1917; The Dalles, 1918; Milton, 1919; Pendleton, 1920; Baker, 1921; Elgin, 1922; Heppner, 1923; La Grande, 1924; Milton, 1925; The Dalles, 1926; Pendleton, 1927; and Baker, 1928.

A new departure from the usual order of convention program was begun in 1918. At a mass meeting of all the cooperating boards held on August 2, 1917, it was decided thereafter to "turn the forenoon sessions into lecture periods of approximately one hour each, having one lecturer from the East for one address each morning and evening, using the best available talent for other morning periods, and using the afternoons for whatsoever convention program each organization may wish." This form of program has been in use in a modified way ever since. For several years a Leadership Training School has been conducted as a part of the morning sessions.

With the breaking out of the war our pulpits were drained as well as the pews. In the service from Oregon there appears the following names of ministers: F. T. Porter, Salem; W. A. Elkins, Lebanon; Willard Hayes, student; Chris. J. Jensen, Student; James H. McCallum, student; Frank L. Purnell, student; Ralph L. Putnam, student; Gottlieb Schmid, student; Frank A. Wood, student; Earl M. Smith, student; J. Carlos Ghormley, Wasco; Horace Kessler, student; Mark J. Bunce, student; Roy Samuel, student; Ernest Samuel, student; Robert C. Strong, student; Raymond C. Smith, student; Wm. Phene Sutton, student. All honor to these men!

In May, 1918, what was known as the "Emergency Drive" was with us. It was an emergency relief for the general missionary work in all the world. Consequent upon the high prices that had arisen on mission fields as an effect of the war a serious deficiency had arisen in the mission treasury. Oregon was apportioned $20,000 and went gloriously "over the top."

In these days of compromise and "peace at any price" people sometimes feel the necessity for declaring themselves. The convention of 1919 did this in regards to movements for unity in a well written resolution. H. E. Rossell was the chairman of the committee that introduced the resolution. It is a classic and deserves to live on the pages of our history in Oregon. It was as follows:

"That we look with favor upon any movement for the union of God's people and the answer of our Saviour's prayer that is consistent with the divine authority as plainly revealed in the Gospel of His grace, and that we pledge ourselves anew to the great plea for the restoration of the church of the New Testament; and that in these days of unrest we plead more earnestly for the basic condition of membership in His church as faith in the Lord Jesus Christ, confession of that worthy name before men, repentance from the heart of all sin, and baptism into the name of the Father, Son and Holy Spirit, followed by a holy life; and that we reassert our blood bought liberty in Christ to go anywhere and everywhere without hindrance to proclaim the gospel of His love."

With this strong pronouncement none can accuse Oregon of being disloyal to the "plea."

A venture in the tract publishing business was taken at the convention in 1920. A fund of $150 was raised, and three tracts were ordered published: "Christian Baptism," by M. Howard Fagan; "Modern Substitutes," by

W. L. Myers; and "Christian Stewardship," by C. F. Swander. The plan was to sell these tracts and keep the money going round and round publishing other tracts. It was a good plan, but its weakness was in the fact that people wouldn't buy the tracts. The venture was a financial failure. The State Board paid a deficit on the printing of the first edition and they still have a large number of tracts unsold. Publishing tracts is a good form of missionary work, but its success cannot be predicted if the tracts must be sold.

In the spring of 1919 the State Board bought a Multigraph at a cost of about $450. It has proved to be a tremendous asset to the state work. Practically all the printing for the State Board has been done on this machine since its purchase, thus lessening the cost of the Board's printing bill. In addition to an actual saving on printing costs it has permitted a volume of printed matter that would otherwise have been prohibitive. The saving in necessary printing alone has more than paid the original cost of the machine and all its upkeep. No better material investment was ever made by the State Board.

In September of 1919 the State Board took another forward step—the opening of a down town office for headquarters and workshop for the Board. Hitherto the Secretary had conducted all his work from his home, and the Bible School Superintendent had done the same. With the rental of an office the two officers were located in the same room much to their mutual advantage. The office was opened in the Panama building, Portland, at the corner of Third and Alder Streets, where it remains to the time of this writing.

By 1922 the tabernacle roof was getting in a bad state of repair. One could stand within and see the stars through the holes in the roof. The rain was coming through so badly that seats and floor were becoming damaged. It was decided to reroof the building at once. A call was made for money and more than $900 was pledged at the convention. This was followed up with an active campaign for improvements money. By the close of the convention in 1923 the roof had been placed on the tabernacle, one on the restaurant, new sides placed on the restaurant, and sundry other improvements on the grounds and buildings, at a cost of $2,226.77, with all bills paid in full.

Very early in the history of the Turner meetings it was deemed advisable to "take a collection" at the gate as people passed in. While no "admission charge" was made, yet each person was expected to deposit at least ten cents in the box. It virtually amounted to an admission fee and people so understood it. The gate fee never was popular, but it got the money. In 1916 the gate fee was suspended and in its place an offering was taken on Sundays. The experiment was a financial disaster, and the gate fee reappeared the next year. Its presence became increasingly distasteful, however, and in 1920 the State Board decided that the loss of money was better than the gate fee, so it was "abolished henceforth and forevermore." The Sunday offerings since that time have more than equalled the gate fees of former years. There is no intention of returning to the former practice.

The lack of laymen at the conventions has been a sore spot in our annual gatherings. In 1924 it was decided by the joint program committee to attempt a laymen's session, giving Monday afternoon over wholly to the men to conduct and control. A splendid session was held that year, presided over by Ira C. Powell, of Monmouth, who was enthusiastic in its behalf. But it did not seem to be popular and it has been attempted only once since.

One of the deplorable conditions that has hovered over our convention grounds was the gradual loss of our trees. One by one the giant firs succumbed to some insect or disease until it became apparent that the time would come when we would have no shade at all. In 1923 the State Board began to plant maples on the grounds. Success attended this in goodly measure. The time will not be far distant when convention comers may disport themselves 'neath the cool shade of giant Norway maples.

At the convention in 1924 the greatest forward step ever taken by Oregon disciples was inaugurated. At the East Oregon Convention that year resolutions were presented memorializing the Turner convention to set a missionary goal that was worthy our greatness as a people and the greatness of our plea. They suggested $25,000 per year as a goal. The convention at Turner unanimously adopted it. While the goal has never yet been reached it is a lode stone that has moved the people to greater contributions than ever before.

The convention of 1927 was denominated the "Diamond Anniversary of state gatherings" because it was 75 years since that first meeting at McCoy in 1852. For five years the matter of a fitting celebration was kept before the churches and in 1927 extra efforts were put forth in the matter of both the program and the crowd. The attendance was record breaking, while the world renowned evangelist, Charles Reign Scoville, was present as the convention speaker to make it a great program. In preparation for this "Diamond Anniversary" a song was written as Oregon's State Song, set to the tune of "Loyalty to Christ." It was suggested by W. L. Myers and the words were arranged by C. F. Swander. It follows:

OREGON FOR CHRIST

The Christian Church today, Is mingling in the fray,
    For Oregon, Oregon, Oregon for Christ;
Some twenty thousand strong, We cheerily march along,
    Thru Oregon, Oregon, Oregon with Christ!

CHORUS—"On to victory!   On to victory!"
        Cries the great Commander, "On!"
          We'll move at His command, We'll soon possess the
            land,
        Of Oregon, Oregon, Oregon for Christ.

Then over hill and plain, We sing the glad refrain,
    Of "Oregon, Oregon, Oregon for Christ!"
The breakers join the song, Of right against the wrong,
    'Tis "Oregon, Oregon, Oregon for Christ!"

        Chorus

The Sunday Schools will all, Join in the gospel call,
    Of "Oregon, Oregon, Oregon for Christ!"
Our ranks are growing fast, The work we do will last,
    'Tis Oregon, Oregon, Oregon for Christ.

        Chorus

The C. E. forces too, Ring out the watchword true,
    Of "Oregon, Oregon, Oregon for Christ!"
We'll go thru all the land, A happy conq'ring band,
    'Tis Oregon, Oregon, Oregon for Christ.

        Chorus

Our lives we'll consecrate, To our beloved state,
  'Tis Oregon, Oregon, Oregon for Christ;
His gospel we'll proclaim, Thruout the state's domain,
  'Tis Oregon, Oregon, Oregon for Christ.

Chorus

The Diamond Jubilee, Will crown a victory,
  For Oregon, Oregon, Oregon and Christ;
We'll chord the harps of heaven, In nineteen-twenty seven,
  For Oregon, Oregon, Oregon and Christ.

Chorus

CHAPTER VII

THE GROWTH OF THE CAUSE

In this chapter we shall attempt to show as completely as possible a roster of all the churches that are now, and have been, in the state. It would be too voluminous to give a detailed history of each congregation even if we had such a record, though some are richly deserving of it. We shall attempt to show as accurately as we can, from the information available, the date of organization and whether it still lives. Bold faced type indicates that the church so designated no longer lives. Occasionally a brief comment is thrown in.

1846

"**On the Yamhill**," somewhere in the northern part of Polk county. The exact location is lost to history. Even the name by which it was known, if it had such, is lost. It lives in history only by the phrase, "On the Yamhill." It was organized by Amos Harvey. His donation land claim was in Polk county near the present village of McCoy. This was the FIRST congregation of Christians only in the state of Oregon, and was composed of 13 members. The date was the month of March. Mrs. W. G. Armsworthy, of Wasco, Oregon, is a descendant of Amos Harvey.

"**School District No. 1**," was the first Christian Church organized in Yamhill county, according to the testimony of F. M. York, who had it from the lips of one who participated in it, G. L. Rowland. Saturday, August 1,

1846, is given as the date, Vincent Snelling as the organizer, and the Ruel Olds place as the exact location. "The first man baptized by immersion was in the Yamhill river just below the Andy Hembree place, on Sunday August 2, 1846. The man baptized was Wm. Higgins, a son-in-law of V. Snelling."

"On the Clackamas," was a church organized by John Foster. The day and month have not been preserved, hence it is impossible to tell whether it was the second, or third, congregation organized in the state. The exact location is also lost to history, but it was doubtless not far from the present town of Gladstone. The fact of its existence is known, however, and that is the important fact for a history.

1847

"Blackhawk Schoolhouse," six miles northwest of McMinnville, was organized by Aaron Payne. This church was the progenitor of the present McMinnville church, and Mrs. W. L. Warren, who has been a member at McMinnville for many years, is a granddaughter of Aaron Payne.

"Howells Prairie," was the name of a country congregation near Salem. Nothing more is known of it than the fact of its existence.

1848

Damascus, in Clackamas county. This may possibly have been the church organized by John Foster "on the Clackamas" in 1846, but the name of Damascus does not appear until 1848. There is nothing to indicate an identity of the two congregations. The name Damascus appears on the roll of churches as late as 1893.

Luckimute, also in Polk county, was organized by H. M. Waller on the second Sunday in October. We are indebted for the accuracy of these two items to a little blank book once owned by H. M. Waller, in which these two items stand as the sole entry upon its pages. The book is now prized as a keepsake by Mr. and Mrs. E. R. Huston, Heppner, Oregon, to whom we are immediately indebted for the information.

Rickreal, in Polk county, was organized by Glen O. Burnett, on the first Sunday in May. James McBride and H. M. Waller assisted in setting the congregation in order.

1849

No new names appear on the roll this year.

1850

Pleasant Hill, Lane county, is the only name we have found for 1850. It was organized on August 4. Elijah Bristow was the prime mover in its organization. The church is still alive and active and bears the distinction of being the oldest Christian church in the state still existing on its original location. Until the ''flu ban'' in 1918 this church carried the record of never having missed a communion service since its organization. ''This locality is distinguished by having given to Lane county its first dwelling house, first schoolhouse, first church, first cemetery, and the first wedding ceremony.''

1851

Bethany, in Marion county, a little way west of Silverton. Its name appears on the record for the last time in

1893. The old building is still standing in a fair state of preservation. It was erected in 1858 and is now the oldest standing Christian church house in the state. It had a long and honorable record as a church.

Roland, about three miles north of Lafayette. This was doubtless either a schoolhouse church, or a farmside congregation. Dr. James McBride was their most frequent minister.

1852

Central, in Linn county, about seven miles east of Albany. This has always been a purely rural church. The church was organized by the Powell brothers and for many years was one of the strong churches of the brotherhood. Its name was not taken off the list until 1925, but for several years previously they had ceased to report and did not hold services of any character. The name was carried on the list for some time in the fond hope that it would "come back." With the advent of the automobile, and the organization of a church at Crabtree close by, there is very little reason for the existence longer of a congregation at Central. Like other institutions, and like human beings, it served its purpose and did it splendidly, and has now passed on to live only in the memories of those who loved the cause.

Sheridan, in Yamhill county. It still lives and prospers. No record is left of its origin but it has made important history during later years.

1853

Hillsboro **(Hillsborough),** Washington county. The author has reason to believe that the date was actually much earlier than this but this is the first reference to it in the records. The original spelling of the name is given in parenthesis.

Shaddon Schoolhouse, about a mile and a half northwest of McMinnville. This was the Blackhawk church moved to a more convenient location, and it was the immediate progenitor of the McMinnville church.

1854

Bethel, Polk county, near the present town of McCoy. Glen O. Burnett organized the church and named it after old Bethel church in Missouri. For a number of years before its demise it was ministered to by the veteran I. N. Mulkey. Its name appeared on the record last in 1916, but for several years previously its doors had remained closed. It rendered three score years of glorious service to the cause of Christianity and its name will go down in our history as a church that "though dead, yet it speaketh."

Big Muddy, "near to the dividing line between Linn and Lane counties, September, 1854, with 11 members." This is like an epitaph upon a tombstone—just a brief word of existence.

South Fork, location undiscovered. It is mentioned as a church in reports to the *Christian-Evangelist* for that year. There are many "south forks," "north forks," and "middle forks," in the geography of that day. There is no ear mark by which this particular South Fork is distinguished from all the rest.

Wallace Butte, in Lane county, was organized in the month of June with 14 members. The length of its life is not known.

1855

Aumsville, in Marion county, was organized as the Mill Creek church in 1855. It still lives in name. That veteran disciple, H. C. Porter, has valiantly maintained a Bible school through the years of its existence. The story is told elsewhere in this history of the preacher who advertised that he would preach the funeral of this church; but when he went to perform his task there were not enough present to act as pall bearers, and the burial was indefinitely postponed.

Amity, in Yamhill county. It has maintained an active existence all through the years and still flourishes.

Chehalem, in Yamhill county. A report in the Millennial Harbinger for that year is the evidence of its existence.

Clear Lake, in Lane county, in the month of June, with 14 members.

Coles Valley, in Douglas county, was a small congregation ministered to by E. G. Browning.

Lafayette, in Yamhill county, is another church reported in the Millennial Harbinger for that year.

Looking Glass Prairie, in Douglas county, was organized in June, with 7 members. Mary Preston was a charter member. A church building was erected, which burned down some years later. The congregation ceased then. During recent years a mission point has been maintained there ministered to by preachers in the county.

McMinnville, Yamhill county, comes into being this year under this name. It was the Shaddon schoolhouse congregation that was moved into town; and the Shaddon schoolhouse congregation was the Blackhawk congregation moved to the Shaddon schoolhouse. So the real birth of the church known since as the McMinnville church was back in 1847 at the Blackhawk schoolhouse. The honor of being the oldest living church in the state lies between McMinnville and Pleasant Hill. If age is to be determined by continuance in a settled location then the honors go to Pleasant Hill; but if age of organization, without regard to location, is the determining factor then McMinnville is the champion by a full three years.

Myrtle Creek, in Douglas county. Reports in the papers indicate the existence of a church there at that early date. However, it died and was later reorganized. The present church carries the date of 1888 as its birthday.

Spring Valley, was located either in Yamhill county or Washington county. A meeting was held there sometime during the year with 16 baptisms and 31 added otherwise. John Murphey, Glen O. Burnett, and James McBride were the evangelistic team.

1856

Dallas, in Polk county. Its early history is not available, but it remains one of our strong churches to this day and has had a glorious ministry.

Monmouth, in Polk county, was organized in July, 1856, by a group of men who had come to Oregon for the express purpose of organizing a Christian College. Monmouth was the location chosen. "According to the first clerk's book, which has been carefully preserved, 35 pioneers met in July, 1856, and organized a 'Christian congregation; the Bible the only infallible rule of faith and practice.' Among the charter members were Elijah Davidson, John E. Murphy, Albert Lucas, Squire S. Whitman and others.

When the church was organized meetings were held in a little square schoolhouse which stood on the old public square.'' T. F. Campbell, for many years President of Christian College, was its minister also for many years.

Winchester, in Douglas county, was cared for by S. D. Evans, a ''lay preacher.''

1857

Abaca, location unknown. Its existence is revealed in the files of the *Christian-Evangelist* for that year. Another historian suggests that this is a corrupted spelling (perhaps a typist's error in composing) of the name Abiqua, which appears as a church on the list first in 1891.

Rainier, in Columbia county, was organized by a Brother Huntington. This church was evidently not long lived. Rainier is now a considerable town; it is gratifying to know that the gospel once had root there; we look upon the place with a longing that it may be so again.

Silver Creek, in Marion county, appears in a report to the *Christian-Evangelist* for October, 1857. Rather reliable information suggests that this was possibly only another name for the old Bethany church.

1858

Salem First, in Marion county. The news reports mention that A. V. McCarty located with this church in that year, so its organization was doubtless earlier, though we have no means of determining just when. It still lives, is one of the influential congregations in the capital city, and one of the stronger churches among Christian Churches in the state.

South Yamhill, in Yamhill county somewhere, as shown by reports in the papers. It was doubtless somewhere on the South Yamhill river.

1859

Scio, in Linn county. It still lives. For a brief period it tried the experiment of federation, which failed as all such efforts do. They have some souls which are loyal to the "Plea."

1860

There is no record of churches organized in 1860.

1861

Hebron, in Lane county. Like many other small churches Hebron has had a halting career. Purely rural in its character it has declined and died, again revived, and the process repeated. Its last reorganization was on December 24, 1922, by C. C. Morgan. It still lives and is ministered to regularly by students from Eugene Bible University.

1862

Eugene First, in Lane county, on March 26. It is now the largest and most influential church in the state. It bears the distinction of having the only set of chimes in any church in the state, being installed in 1925 under the leadership of Elijah V. Stivers.

1863

Antioch, definitely appears on the list, but exact location is not known.

Centerville, location unknown. Records of the state meeting at Eola that year bear the names of delegates from Centerville.

Coast Fork, location unknown.

Eola, in Polk county. A state meeting was held there in 1863, which would make it seem certain that the church was organized at an earlier date. There is no means of identifying an exact date so we are placing it in the year when first mentioned. The old building stood until 1924 when it was torn down. A picture was taken of it before razing it and that now hangs upon the wall of the state office. The old pulpit desk was taken out and is preserved as a relic in the tabernacle at Turner.

Farmington, in Washington county. This was one of the strong early day churches. Its name has been off the church roll for many years, but a Sunday school has been maintained there for most of the time. From time to time it has been revived as a preaching point for students of Eugene Bible University.

Harrisburg, in Linn county, was organized on November 7, by John E. Murphy, with 31 members. The old building, erected in 1870, is still standing and giving service. "Official church records were seemingly lost, but when the old seats were torn out, on a board from the back of one of the seats was found the following inscription, written with a carpenter's heavy pencil: 'Began to build this home in June, 1869, finished on the 17th day of March, 1870, and was dedicated on the first Sunday in April, 1870. The builders were Alfred Simmons and John Martin, and others who helped were Willoughby Churchill, Thomas Roach and Mr. Humphreys.' "

Harris Bridge, location unknown.

Salt Creek, in Polk county. Only an obscure reference gives this church a place in the record.

Upper Muddy, probably in Lane county.

1864-1873

There is a long silence during these years. It could not have been a silence of activity and church organization, but a silence of records. Those pioneers were too busy making history to write it. Nowhere have we been able to locate data concerning churches during this time. Much to our regret we must pass over it. It is the belief of the author that some of the churches listed later on belong in reality to this period. But the historian cannot record events according to his beliefs. He must list them according to the best information.

1874

Halsey, in Linn county. This church still lives and has had a part in kingdom affairs beyond the natural expectations for a small village church. Most notable of her contributions to the kingdom was the gift of Goldie Ruth Wells to mission work in Africa. She has also sent out young men into the ministry of the Lord. When the roll of churches is called up there Halsey will be among those of whom it will be said, ''For from you hath sounded forth the word of the Lord.''

1875

Independence, in Polk county, was organized on April 4. This church still lives. It has passed through deep waters many times, but always there have been the faithful few who kept the light burning.

1876

Elkton, in Douglas county, was organized in the month of December. For many years the banner of the church floated over this community. Then the cause weakened and died. The burning of the church building in later years was the final blow. It was finally reorganized in September, 1925, and continues to this day.

1877

Yamhill, formerly known as North Yamhill, was organized in the month of July. The congregation still lives and has had an existence that they may well be proud of.

1878

Drain, in Douglas county, was organized in the month of August. This small church has demonstrated that a pastor can be kept in a small village. Under the leadership of Dr. T. M. White in recent years it has had a remarkable history.

1879

Portland First, in Multnomah county, was organized on February 9. This church was the first missionary objective the Christian Church ever had in the state. The beginning days were difficult and slow, but now they have a membership of more than 1,200 souls, with a property that is worth $150,000.

1880

There is no record of church organization this year.

1881

Helix, in Umatilla county, in the month of April.

Junction City, in Lane county. This congregation has been helpful to the kingdom in a material way.

Stayton, in Marion county, was organized in **March**. This church has made a good record.

1882

Fairview, in Lane county.

Liberty, location unknown. The nation loves to honor the graves of its unknown dead. Christians should honor the names of these unknown churches—unknown except in name.

Springfield, in Lane county. This congregation has made steady progress during the years.

Trent, in Lane county. It died and was resurrected by T. S. Handsaker on December 7, 1913.

1883

Albany, in Linn county. This is one of the important county seat towns in the state, and the church has kept pace with the town.

Brownsville, in Linn county. It is still doing a good work.

Carlton, in Yamhill county, in the month of July. The church still lives and is active.

Corvallis, in Benton county, in the month of October. Corvallis is the seat of the Oregon Agricultural College, and is, therefore, an important locality. The church has made a consistent effort to reach the college folk with a reasonable degree of success. It would appear from historical records that the organization at this time did not maintain permanently, for the organization that flourishes today bears the birth date of February, 1890, at which time an auxiliary to the C. W. B. M. was organized in the home of W. W. Bristow. The church organization was not effective until October 15, 1891.

Clackamas, in Clackamas county.

Coquille, in Coos county. At the present time this is our leading congregation on Coos Bay.

Crawfordsville, in Linn county. This is purely a rural community. The church has been disbanded and reorganized many times. It is not now living.

Forest Grove, in Washington county, in the month of September, by Peter R. Burnett. It is strong and virile to this day.

Gaston, in Yamhill county.

Hedrix, location unknown.

Mt. Pleasant, location unknown.

Oak Creek, location unknown, probably in Linn county.

Oretown, location unknown. Its name would indicate a mining camp. If so it would probably be somewhere in the mountains.

St. Helens, in Columbia county. This organization did not survive long. For many years the cause was dormant. A love for the place was cherished in the heart of Sister Perkins, of Drain, which caused her to pledge $200 for the establishment of the work there again. G. W. Hay, pastor at Astoria, accepted the challenge and laid siege to it in August and September, 1927. After six weeks' effort, in which he was assisted by J. F. Cunningham, of Beaverton, a church was organized of 85 members. It is now a promising work.

1884

Hood River Valley, in Hood River county, in the month of September. This is purely a rural community and this was the first Christian Church organized in that Valley. It still lives and sees the work organized in two other places in the valley.

Medford, in Jackson county, November 22. It is now one of the largest churches in southern Oregon. It was the author's pleasure to deliver the memorial sermon at their 40th anniversary.

1885

No organizations on record for this year.

1886

Milton, in Umatilla county. This church has had a wonderful career and has become one of the strong churches in the state.

1887

East Portland, in Multnomah county. This was the second effort to establish the work in Portland. L. F. Stephens and H. B. Morgan were prominent in the attempt. It disbanded on July 3, 1895.

Holly, in Linn county. This was another rural church, disbanded and reorganized many times. It is not now living, but the old church building stands and there is an occasional service in it. In the shifting of communities this neighborhood is served quite well by the churches at Sweet Home, Lebanon and Brownsville.

Perrydale, in Polk county. This, too, is a rural community, but one that has demonstrated the possibility and wisdom of rural organizations. Though small they have always had a staunch clientele.

Silverton, in Marion county. It is now recognized as one of the strong churches in the state. Though situated in a community that is strongly Catholic and foreign the church has entrenched itself strongly.

1888

Grants Pass, in Josephine county, in the month of January. It is now one of our strong congregations in the state.

Prineville, in Crook county. It did not long survive this organization. The records show that Dillard Holman reorganized them in 1890 or 1891. Their building burned in 1927 which completely caused the assembling to cease. The church lives in name only.

1889

Roseburg, in Douglas county, on May 26, in the home of C. A. Sehlbrede, with 14 charter members. For seven years the congregation did without a minister while struggling with a debt, but during that time they never failed to spread the Lord's table. The church is now reckoned in the front rank of Christian churches in the state. They erected a new building in 1928 which was dedicated on April 29.

Wasco, in Sherman county. This is another church in a small community that has not ceased to survive through all vicissitudes.

1890

Cottage Grove, in Lane county. The writer heard it said of this church once that it was the most spiritual church in the state. Whether or not the statement be 100 per cent true it speaks well of a congregation that makes such an impression on people.

Halfway, Baker county, on December 26. This is a rural community, for many years isolated from civilization nearly 60 miles from a railroad. Now it has a road within 12 miles. There have been times when the Cause swept the entire valley. There are still many members scattered about who do not affiliate. The Christian Church has made a tremendous impress on Pine Valley, as the community is known.

La Grande, in Union county. La Grande is one of the important towns in East Oregon. The church has grown apace with the town and, at this writing, is drawing plans for a new building that will adequately house a growing work.

Thurston, in Lane county, on April 6. For most of its life it has been a student point. It may seem to some of these rural churches that they haven't amounted to much in the kingdom; but, if they would only stop to count up the number of preachers they have made, they would think otherwise. Many of these student points have really made a larger contribution to the kingdom in their preparation of preachers than have some of the larger churches.

1891

The following names appear first on the list in 1891. Without doubt some of them were organized earlier, but there is no data by which we can exactly locate them. We give them here as the best effort to locate them:

Athena, in Umatilla county. This is a small community, but the church reached considerable proportions at one time. The removal of many of the members has left the church weak in members though it still remains faithful to the cause.

Abiqua, in Marion county. (See Abaca in 1857). The Abiqua Creek (Alberqua on the present day maps) flows a short distance from Scotts Mills. It is likely that the Abiqua Church merged into the Scotts Mills church of later date and thus lost its identity.

Blockhouse, in Morrow county.

Canyonville, in Douglas county.

Cheshire, in Lane county.

Coburg, in Lane county. It was reorganized in 1903 and is doing splendid work today.

Currinsville, in Clackamas county. This is near Estacada and probably lost its identity in that church at a later date.

Eagle Creek, in Clackamas county.

Eightmile, in Morrow county. This has been a preaching point many times since its disbandment, but the church has been gone for many years.

Fir Grove, in Lane county.

George Hall, in Union county.

Gold Hill, in Jackson county.

Hadleyville, in Lane county. This has been an occasional preaching point for students from Eugene Bible University.

Jasper, in Lane county. It was reorganized in 1905.

Leaburg, in Lane county.

Long Tom, in Lane county.

Lorane, in Lane county. This church died as an organized body, but it was restored as an active preaching point in 1926 and was fully reorganized as a church October 30, 1927.

Lost Valley, in Lane county.

Mabel, in Lane county.

Mill City, in Linn county. This church soon died, but in July, 1926, Teddy Leavitt held a meeting that resulted in the organization of a church of nearly 200 members. It is now a flourishing church.

Molalla, in Clackamas county. A small "anti" congregation exists there now.

Monroe, in Benton county.

Monitor, in Marion county.

Oakland, in Douglas county. It was reorganized in 1908. It has had many experiences as a church. They once went into a "federation" but a faithful few refused to federate. It was some years before they fully recovered from the experiment, but they are now a strong country church.

Pendleton, in Umatilla county. It was born in the month of August. It is situated in one of the fine towns of eastern Oregon and is one of our strong churches.

Point Terrace, in Lane county.

Sycamore, in Multnomah county.

South Springs, in Morrow county.

Sand Ridge, in Union county.

Union Hill, in Marion county.

Walton, in Lane county.

1892

Canby, in Clackamas county. It has been reorganized a number of times. In 1917 the State Secretary found its light almost gone. He held a meeting, set them in order and located a pastor. They were faithful until the "flu ban" struck a year later. They did not recover from that. In 1925 the Eugene Bible University took title to their property for the consideration of putting it in repair. It then became an active preaching point for students again.

Dufur, in Wasco county, in the month of July. This has been a strong congregation in its day. Dufur was once the center of a growing fruit section. Commercial reverses came that took out a large portion of the population and the strength of the church was cut proportionately. However, the church still burns its light brightly.

Falls City, in Polk county, in the month of March. Falls City has been a lumber town. It has always been a live village and the church has kept pace with the community. For the most part it has been ministered to by students and they have acquitted themselves well.

The Dalles, Wasco county. This church was organized by J. W. Jenkins, one of the pioneer ministers of Eastern Oregon. It has become a strong church.

Tillamook, in Tillamook county. For many years the New Testament plea has had a strong hold in Tillamook. The congregation has not been strong financially, and because of that they have struggled bravely under a huge debt. They have a good building and have made progress.

1893

Dayton, in Yamhill county. Dayton is "over churched" so far as organizations go. Consequently all churches have had a struggle. Howbeit, the Christian Church has always kept open house, and for the most time they have had a minister. They number some staunch disciples in their midst.

Enterprise, in Wallowa county, in the month of February. This congregation tried the experiment of federation, tying up in an agreement with three other congregations for a period of five years. They righteously lived up to their contract, but when the agreement closed it was necessary to send in the state evangelist to gather up the fragments and build them into a Church of Christ again. Every federation experiment in the state has proved a failure.

Heppner, in Morrow county. This was the home town of J. V. Crawford, a pioneer Oregon preacher who is mentioned on previous pages. His connections were largely the secret of Heppner's present strength as a church.

Portland Third, in Multnomah county. The name was changed later to Rodney Avenue, and in 1921 it was merged with the Woodlawn congregation to form the Mallory Avenue Church of Christ and located at the corner of Mallory Avenue and Alberta Street. David Wetzel organized the old Third Church.

The following names appear for the first time on the 1893 list but it seems probable that some of them at least existed earlier than this date:

Astoria, in Clatsop county. This organization was short-lived. In 1918 the State Board sent their evangelist, R.

L. Dunn, to Astoria with instructions to stay long enough to build a church or demonstrate that it couldn't be done. He organized the church. Various fortunes have come to it but through all of them there has been steady progress. The disastrous fire that burned up the business part of the town in 1921 was a severe setback to the church, but it survived it. This was the fourth effort at organizing the cause in Astoria and it was accomplished on May 1, 1918.

Camas Valley, in Douglas county.

Central Point, in Jackson county. It was reorganized March 4, 1903, and still lives.

Gales Creek, in Washington county.

Hood River, in Hood River county. It was reorganized October 3, 1905. The church has always had a struggle but it has steadily grown. Some of our best preachers have been numbered among its ministers.

Irving, in Lane county. The old church building was finally turned over to the Eugene Bible University.

Lancaster, in Lane county.

Newberg, in Yamhill county. This effort did not long continue. On April 9, 1907, it was organized anew as the result of a meeting held by Geo. C. Ritchey. That meeting was held as the outgrowth of an action by the Northwest District Convention a few weeks previously. It is now one of the strong churches in the Valley with an up-to-date building.

Oregon City, in Clackamas county. This congregation did not survive. This was one of the hard places in the state to get a foothold. Time and time again the effort was made only to be defeated. Early in 1926 the State Board arranged with Paul DeF. Mortimore, pastor at Gladstone, to hold weekly services in a hall for the faithful ones to be found there. The State Board paid the expenses incidental thereto. This led up to a meeting by Teddy Leavitt in the fall and on October 4, 1926 an organization was affected that has since maintained and grown. The State Board helped to pay for the meeting and counts it one of their best investments. The church has been meeting in a hall but they are now preparing to burst out from the shell and assume the place of power and influence in the community they deserve.

Walterville, in Lane county.

Williams, location unknown.

1894

There is no record of churches organized in 1894.

1895

Pioneer, in Marion county.

Portland, Woodlawn, in Multnomah county, in October by J. F. Ghormley, then pastor of the First Church. In 1921 they merged with the Rodney Avenue Church to form the Mallory Avenue Church of Christ.

Richland, in Baker county. This church still lives.

Union, in Union county. After a series of scandalous troubles the church house burned down and the church died. There is hope that it may live again.

1896

Elmira, in Lane county, in the month of January.

Scotts Mills, in Marion county. A reorganization on January 17, 1915, is alive at this writing.

1897

Franklin, in Lane county, in August. This church has sometimes been known as Smithfield.

1898

Alvadore, in Lane county. In its beginning days it was a purely crossroads church, and was known as Fern Ridge. When the railroad went through a station close by was named Alvadore and the name of the church was finally changed to that designation.

Ashland, in Jackson county, was born on April 19. It has been weak in finance but strong in faith.

Elgin, in Union county. This church has evangelized the whole country round about. At one time there were recorded more than 250 members in the Elgin church, but the working unit was much smaller. It is evidence of consecrated zeal in spreading the Word, however.

Kingston, in Linn county. Kingston is situated just across the river from Stayton. Stayton had the strong church, but Kingston had a railroad. The Kingston church was formed by a group of people who were members of the church at Stayton but who lived on the Kingston side of the river. Perhaps, too, there were optimistic visions that Kingston would outdistance Stayton in the race as a city. But the church did not long continue.

1899

The following names appear on the list for the first time this year, yet it seems probable that some of them, at least, existed before that date:

Alicel, in Union county. Alicel is not much more than

a suburb of La Grande, hence it is hardly to be expected that a church could well exist there. This organization died and was born again in October, 1910. But that did not endure.

Baker, in Baker county. We have no record how long this effort lasted. In the last part of 1909 the State Secretary received an appeal from a Ladies' Aid Society to "Come over and help us." He went and held a week's meeting which resulted in the reorganization of the cause with 47 members on January 2, 1910. It has been a husky child ever since.

Echo, location unknown with certainty. It cannot be positively identified with the Echo in Umatilla county.

Glenada, location unknown.

Lebanon, in Linn county. This was an abortive effort but in January, 1908, a reorganization was effected which has survived.

Lostine, in Wallowa county. This church still lives but it has not supported regular preaching for a long time. Their permanency was assured by the gift of a building for church purposes by Sister M. E. McCubbin.

Lyonsville, location unknown.

Mosier, in Wasco county. This church has existed, and saved souls, for many years without any other ministry than that of the eldership or an occasional meeting. They have had a virile eldership.

Newbridge, in Baker county.

Noble, located on the Crooked Finger Ferry in Marion county.

Parkersville, in Lane county.

Pilot Rock, in Umatilla county.

Yoncalla, in Douglas county. It was later reorganized but did not survive that. Again in June of 1928 Garland Hay held a seven weeks' meeting that resulted in a church of 74 members.

1900

The following names appear for the first time on the 1900 list. For the most part they are of unknown location and many of them existed only for a short time, and some of them perhaps in name only. But the appearance of their names on the list is an evidence of the preaching of the gospel and saving of souls:

Alpha, location unknown.

Condon, in Gilliam county. It is quite certain that the congregation reported here was more or less identical with an "anti" church that is known to have existed there since.

Cove, in Union county.

Deer Creek, location unknown, perhaps in Douglas county.

Dilley, in Washington county.

Dusty, location unknown.

Hay Creek, location unknown.

Haystack, in Crook county.

Herman, location unknown.

Lakeview, in Lake county.

New Pine Creek, Lake county. This church existed until late in this decade.

Oak Hill, location unknown.

Pleasant Valley, location unknown.

Shoestring Valley, location unknown.

Star, location unknown.

Turner, in Marion county. The building was burned and the congregation disbanded. In 1919 a meeting was held by Ralph Putnam in the Presbyterian church which resulted in a splendid organization. In 1925 Mrs. Cornelia A. Davis built a memorial church house for the congregation which cost upwards of $40,000.

1901

Ivison, location unknown.

Nashville, in Lincoln county, in August, by J. B. Lister.

Riverton, in Coos county.

Rock Point, in Marion county.

Woodburn, in Marion county. This may be the remains of the old Monitor congregation. It still lives.

1902

Myrtle Point, in Coos county, on November 24.

Riddle, in Douglas county. It died and was organized again in July, 1927, by Wm. R. Baird and Walter Stram.

1903

North Santiam, in Marion county. A forlorn church house is all that indicates the presence of a church there in former years.

Portland Central, in Multnomah county, November 23, by J. F. Ghormley. This was the second attempt to organize the cause on the East side. A monumental stone building was erected at the corner of East 20th and Salmon Streets. Financial difficulties discouraged the leaders and they disbanded in 1915. The new East Side church was born out of its residue. The stone building was finally bought up by the Baptists.

1904

There is no record of organization in 1904, but it is quite certain that some of the churches located elsewhere on the calendar belong to this date.

1905

Marshfield, in Coos county.

Portland Sellwood, in Multnomah county. This little church has had a colorful history. Much of its life it has spent in halls and storerooms. In 1912, with the aid of the City Mission Board, they erected a little home on East 17th and Nehalem Streets. Difficulties arose which caused the congregation to abandon the church house to the bats and they began to keep house again in a rented hall. About 1920 they purchased an abandoned church property at East 8th Street and Spokane Avenue. They improved the property and changed the corporate name of the church to Spokane Avenue Church of Christ, which name it holds to this day.

Santa Clara, in Lane county. This is perhaps the most successful rural church in the state. Its prosperity is due largely to the fact that its close proximity to Eugene, and the prosperity of its membership, gave it the privilege of drawing upon Eugene Bible University for its very best preaching talent among students and faculty.

1906

Berlin, in Linn county.
Grass Valley, in Sherman county.

Ione, in Morrow county. This work was disbanded and reorganized in 1911. It is a flourishing congregation today.

Irrigon, in Morrow county. This has been reorganized several times but without success. A church building stands there as a relic of the Christian Church. The Presbyterians have used it so long that they actually thought they owned it. They would not be convinced even with court records. In later years a considerable controversy arose over it, but nothing was to be gained by contending for the property.

Madras, in Jefferson county.

Odell, in Hood River county. This was disbanded but was reorganized in 1924. It is now a flourishing church.

Phoenix, in Jackson county. The church has disbanded but a meetinghouse is kept open a part of the time.

Portland St. Johns, Multnomah county, on October 28. This has grown to be a strong congregation.

1907

Marcola, in Lane county. N. R. Workman, a resident of the community, has kept the cause alive here.

Portland Kern Park, in Multnomah county, by J. F. Ghormley and E. S. Muckley. This has grown to be one of Portland's influential churches.

Wallowa, in Wallowa county, July 31.

1908

The following churches appear for the first time on the church roll. There are some evidences that they may have existed earlier:

Gooseberry, in Morrow county. J. W. White, a pioneer minister of sainted memory, did much preaching through Morrow county in schoolhouse points. While his work does not live with congregations as memorials, there are hearts in which its influence will never die.

Grizzley, in Crook county.

McKay, in Crook county.

Promise, in Wallowa county. This was afterwards reorganized in 1916, on September 30.

Strawberry, in Morrow county.

Vale, in Malheur county, in April. This has been our lone church in Malheur county for many years.

Wamic, in Wasco county.

1909

Bandon, in Coos county. Reorganized in 1912, but that did not continue.

Bridge, in Coos county. An effort is still being made to carry on a Bible school.

Crabtree, in Linn county, in September.

East Eugene, in Lane county, in May by J. M. Morris. This church is often designated as Fairmount church. It is the second church in Eugene.

Flora, in Wallowa county. It has been reorganized a number of times but it has never succeeded.

Klamath Falls, in Klamath county. A group of people met with the State Secretary in June of that year. They were permanently organized by J. B. Holmes in October. They have grown and now have one of the handsomest buildings in the state.

Laidlaw, in Des Chutes county, in July, by Samuel Gregg.

La Monta, in Crook county.

Silverton Hills, in Marion county, on July 3.

1910

Beaverton, in Washington county, on January 20. This church was disbanded and reorganized by Teddy Leavitt in 1925. It is now one of the strong churches of the community.

Dexter, in Lane county, on January 2. This congregation finally merged with the Trent church and lives now under that name.

Willamina, in Yamhill county on September 11. This church was not long lived but while it did live it gave to the brotherhood one of its strongest preachers, Guy L. Drill.

1911

Culver, in Jefferson county, April 16.

Estacada, in Clackamas county, in September. This was formerly an ''anti'' congregation. A meeting held by the ''progressives'' resulted in the conversion of the church as an organization. A few of the ''anti'' brethren refused, and to this day refuse, to affiliate.

Fossil, in Wheeler county, in November, by G. E. Williams.

Jefferson, in Marion county, in August.

Lower Cove, in Union county, May 1, by Samuel Gregg.

Ontario, in Malheur county, March 26, by G. E. Williams.

Pocahontas, in Baker county, March 5, by Samuel Gregg.

Portland Montavilla, in Multnomah county, January 25, by the First Church through G. K. Berry.

Post, in Crook county, in September, by Samuel Gregg.

Riverview, in Lane county, on June 15. This church was formed by a group of people in the Junction City church who organized in their own community purely for community betterment. They secured a half acre of ground with the intent of building on it, and deeded it to the State Board. Circumstances decreed against their plans and the house was not built. The members were absorbed back into the mother church. In 1927 the State Board sold the property for $75 and put the money into the Permanent Fund.

Spray, in Wheeler county, in October, by G. E. Williams.

Talent, in Jackson county, by W. T. Matlock. For several years this congregation flourished, then many removals caused them to close their house completely.

1912

Bellfountain, in Benton county, January 1.

Creswell, in Lane county, in March.

Evans, in Wallowa county, June 30, by Claude Wingo. A church house was erected and deeded to the State Board. It is not now used.

Wilbur, in Douglas county, September 29, by W. T. Adams.

1913

Corbett, in Multnomah county, September 14, by W. T. Adams. A few years later a "community church" man came into the community and persuaded them to cancel their affiliation with the Christian Church. Accordingly they sent a respectful letter to the State Secretary requesting that their name be taken off the list of churches, which was done. The community idea prevailed for a number of years, but they finally grew away from that idea. When it became apparent that they were again standing for a "Christian only" doctrine the name was restored to the roll. It is a little church

> ". . . . . by the side of the road,
>   Where the stream of men goes by."

Holdman, in Umatilla county, May 25, by A. M. Meldrum.

Kent, in Sherman county, November 16, by A. M. Meldrum. Here is another demonstration of the fact that a church can live and grow if it has a virile internal leadership, notwithstanding the lack of a preacher. For a little more than a year only in its life has this church had a regular preacher. They observe the Lord's Supper every Lord's Day and conduct a Bible School. Occasionally they have a gospel meeting. Yet they have confessions of faith in Jesus. The State Secretary has been called upon to baptize their converts. In 1927 they purchased the Presbyterian meeting house in which they had worshipped since their organization. They plan to erect a comfortable church home some time in the near future.

Liberty Schoolhouse, Morrow county, February 16, by H. A. Van Winkle.

Portland Vernon, Multnomah county, May 8, by J. F. Ghormley. A tabernacle was erected in a good location. After Brother Ghormley finished his work with them J. A. Melton, a layman preacher, carried on the work for a time. It did not succeed and it was dropped. In 1918 R. Tibbs Maxey made an effort to resuscitate the work. The location was soon changed to a hall on Alberta Street. W. E. Lewis, another business man preacher, succeeded Brother Maxey in leadership of the congregation. After consultation with other brethren in the city the little group moved to Englewood district and was organized anew as the Englewood church in 1922.

Rufus, in Sherman county, April 16, by W. F. McCormick.

Rychman, in Lane county, January 19, by E. C. Wigmore.

Trent, in Lane county, December 7, by T. S. Handsaker. This organization was stabilized somewhat by merging with the Dexter congregation.

1914

Fort Rock, in Lake county, May 10, by C. F. Swander and W. T. Matlock. This congregation lived only a short time. But it "found" a most capable and consecrated disciple in the person of George Hockman who lived in a near-by community. After the work at Fort Rock ceased to function he gathered together the people in his own community, Wastina, and conducted a Sunday School and "taught them the way of the Lord more perfectly." He preaches, teaches, and baptizes, thus fulfilling the Great Commission to the letter.

Kellogg, in Douglas county, October 25. This effort finally died, but a reorganization was effected in 1925 which endures to the present day.

Latham, in Lane county.

North Bend, in Coos county, April 12, by Samuel Gregg, State Evangelist. For a dozen years this little congregation held up the banner under most discouraging circumstances. Then the tide turned and they came into their own. In 1927, under the leadership of C. L. Fesler, they completely remodeled their house and thus secured one of the best places of worship in the community.

Salem Court Street, in Marion county, August 30. This congregation was formed by a group of people from the First church who believed that Salem was large enough for two churches. Without the leadership of a pastor they purchased a lot on the corner of 17th and Court streets and erected a bungalow, whence it was familiarly known as the "Bungalow Church." In 1922 they built the foundation for a real temple, but financial troubles came and they were never able to complete but one unit. R. L. Putnam served as pastor for about nine years and did a remarkable work.

1915

Donna, in Lane county. This has never been much more than a preaching point for students from Eugene Bible University, but it served well in that respect.

Lexington, in Morrow county, January 10. This is another weak and struggling church that sometimes thinks it is hardly worth while to continue the struggle. Yet this congregation has given to the brotherhood one of its great men, James A. Pointer.

Portland East Side, in Multnomah county, in November, by A. L. Crim. This congregation was the result of, and continuance of, the old Central Church which disbanded on account of financial difficulties. It has occupied the most strategic district in all the city of Portland. Literally hundreds of disciples have passed through its membership. Unfortunately internal disturbances have shaken it at different times and took out from it scores of good workers. Yet it has always recuperated from these ailments and built up again in a creditable manner. Its location from its birth until the spring of 1928 was on East 12th and Taylor streets, when they sold that property and purchased a lot in Laurelhurst. The church will hereafter be known as Laurelhurst Christian Church.

Redmond, in Des Chutes county, May 4, by George Ramsey.

1916

Maupin, in Wasco county.

Sweet Home, in Linn county. This is a little mountain community. They have fought a good fight—and are winning it.

1917

Bend, in Des Chutes county, May 3, by C. F. Swander, State Secretary. A call came to the state office from H. I. McKim, a laundry driver, who was the son of a preacher, to come over and visit the place. The news of this invitation "leaked out" in Bend, and before the Secretary could respond he had a letter from the Ministerial Association informing him that the community was already over-churched and that his visit was not necessary. He went anyway and, according to the statement of the secretary of the Ministerial body, he found a town of 5,000 population with three English Protestant Churches having a combined membership of about 400 souls. He also found fifty or more "Christians only," 28 of whom he organized into a Church of Christ. A lot was purchased and a little bungalow erected upon it. The work has prospered and demonstrates that the New Testament church will grow in any soil.

1918

Dorena, in Lane county, January 6.

1919, 1920

Three congregations belong to this date, but they are found listed previously because they were reorganizations of previous efforts.

1921

Grande Ronde, in Polk county.

1922

Barlow, in Clackamas county, December 31, by Prof. W. R. Baird. That was a Christmas meeting that resulted in this little church.

Portland Englewood, in Multnomah county, February 22, by W. E. Lewis. This church is the legitimate offspring of the Tabernacle Church in Vernon district in previous years, yet it is not the same organization. It was a work of faith, and it is faith that justifies. This little congregation, without any money, bought a lot and ordered lumber for a modest little house. Other brethren in the city helped them to build a church in a day. The church has prospered and it is now engaging in building plans that will equip it splendidly for serving the community.

1923

Fernvale, in Douglas county, June 27, by Francis M. Arant. This was only a logging camp, and when a church was started in Glendale the next year Fernvale graciously ceded all her rights to organization and gave up the ghost. But the effort served its purpose well.

Garibaldi, in Tillamook county, February 23, by George N. Harness. For a number of years Garibaldi had been a mission point from Tillamook.

North Plains, in Washington county, on November 13, by Gottlieb Schmid and C. F. Swander. The real history of this work goes back beyond that. Seven years before O. P. Burris, while pastor of the Forest Grove church, had made this a preaching station but had not deemed it ready for organization.

Orleans, in Linn county. This congregation was formed by a few brethren from the Corvallis church who lived on the opposite side of the river from the mother congregation. It has maintained its name as a church through the communion service and a Bible School.

Vernonia, in Columbia county, December 23, by Gottlieb Schmid and C. F. Swander. This church owes its existence to a consecrated woman more than to anything else. Mrs. Ethel Ray was a school-teacher in Vernonia who had been reared in the New Testament faith and she could not get away from it, though she let her light shine constantly through another religious body as a channel of service. She persistently kept track of disciples as they came into the community. A group of them asked the State Secretary

to help them. He sent Gottlieb Schmid to hold a meeting
for them. The work has grown amazingly and is destined
to become one of the brightest lights in Columbia county.

1924

Glendale, in Douglas county, January 13, by Francis
Arant. This church is really the continuance of the Fernvale church previously noted. It has not prospered greatly.
In the beginning persecution was bitter and some of the
best workers moved away. But a small group keeps open
house and there are hopes for a brighter future.

Joseph, in Wallowa county, by M. L. Petelle and Gareld
L. Matlock.

Newport, in Lincoln county, December 10, by J. B. Hoag.
Brother Hoag was an aged minister from Ohio who had
come to Newport in behalf of his wife's health. He remained the pastor of the church until his death. From the
beginning the congregation occupied the Baptist church
house. The Baptists had permanently given up the field.
The desire of the Baptists to sell the property, and the
seeming inability of the Church of Christ to purchase it,
caused a lack of confidence as to the permanency of the
new congregation. The State Secretary visited them and
persuaded them that they could buy it and assisted them
in securing title to the property. Immediately the body
commenced to grow.

1925

Alpine, in Morrow county, December 18, by Wallace E.
Jones.

Mehama, in Marion county, June 28, by Merle Applegate and G. W. Hay.

Portland Rosepark, in Multnomah county, in July, by

F. A. Ware. This work had its inception in an effort of
R. Tibbs Maxey some months before to establish the cause
in Rose City Park. Finding insuperable difficulties to that
project he moved out to an abandoned building at the end
of Sandy Boulevard and for some weeks preached
regularly. In July of 1925 F. A. Ware held a meeting
for this unorganized congregation and gave them existence
as a church. They disbanded in 1927.

Seaside, in Clatsop county, October 18, by F. A. Ware.

1926

Curtin, in Douglas county, February 7, by T. M. White.

Powers, in Coos county, in June, by Teddy Leavitt.
The struggle for existence for this little congregation in a
lumbering town was hard. In the early part of 1928 they
made a union with other religious forces in the community.

1927

Glide, in Douglas county, in January, by Henry
Toogood.

Pine City, in Morrow county, February 2, by Eldon L.
Wood.

Portland, Ruby Park, in Multnomah county, February
27, by D. P. Harriman. This congregation was formed
by a group of people from the Montavilla church who went
out as a result of internal disturbance. They maintained
public worship for some time before they resorted to a
separate organization. They continued in the capacity of
a church until February 2, 1928, when they merged with
the East Side church and became an integral part of that
congregation.

Svenson, in Clatsop county, June 6, by G. W. Hay.

Warrenton, in Clatsop county, March 7, by G. W. Hay.

1928

McGlynn, in Lane county, on March 11, by Earl C. Chandler.

From a careful perusal of this list (which must be incomplete) it is seen that the cause has been organized in more than 300 communities in the last fourscore years. Nearly 200 of them have given up the ghost. Some of them were reborn; some of them have passed out of memory except for the name in some obscure report; and some of them lived and prospered from the time of their birth. These church deaths do not mean a decay of the cause. Many of them did their work for their day and their demise is no more to be mourned than the going on of a good man who has lived well his allotted time in this world. In a few cases the loss may well be mourned.

In using this chapter as a reference the reader must not be confused when he does not find a certain church listed in the year in which he *knows* it was organized. The facts are that the year he has in mind was a second, perhaps a third, organization in that community. The rule followed in this chapter is to list the church in the year when it was *first* organized, and make mention there of its final organization. This policy may seemingly depreciate the evangelistic work of certain years in recent times—years that were exceedingly active in organization work, yet the record here apparently does not indicate it for the reason stated above. In order that the reader may the more readily locate a church in this chapter we are here giving a complete alphabetical list of churches with reference to the year in which it will be found in the chapter.

ROSTER OF CHURCHES

With the Years in Which They Are Located in Chapter Seven

Bold faced type indicates churches that have ceased to exist

Abaca (See Abiqua) ___ 1857
Abiqua (See Abaca) ____ 1891
Albany _____ 1883
Alicel _____ 1899
Alpha _____ 1900
Alpine _____ 1925
Alvadore (See Fern
  Ridge) _____ 1898
Amity _____ 1855
Antioch _____ 1863
Ashland _____ 1898
Astoria _____ 1893
Athena _____ 1891
Aumsville _____ 1855

Baker _____ 1899
Bandon _____ 1909
Barlow _____ 1922
Beaverton _____ 1910
Bellfountain _____ 1912
Bend _____ 1917
Berlin _____ 1906
Bethany _____ 1851
Bethel _____ 1854
Big Muddy _____ 1854
Blackhawk Schoolhouse__ 1847
Blockhouse _____ 1891
Bridge _____ 1909
Brownsville _____ 1883

Camas Valley _____ 1893
Canby _____ 1892
Canyonville _____ 1891
Carlton _____ 1883
Central _____ 1852
Centerville _____ 1863
Central Point _____ 1893
Chehalem _____ 1855
Cheshire _____ 1891
"Clackamas, On the" __ 1846
Clackamas _____ 1883
Clear Lake _____ 1855
Coast Fork _____ 1863

Coburg _____ 1891
Coles Valley _____ 1855
Condon _____ 1900
Coquille _____ 1883
Corbett _____ 1913
Corvallis _____ 1883
Cottage Grove _____ 1890
Cove _____ 1900
Crabtree _____ 1909
Crawfordsville _____ 1883
Creswell _____ 1912
Culver _____ 1911
Currinsville _____ 1891
Curtain _____ 1926

Dallas _____ 1855
Damascus _____ 1848
Dayton _____ 1893
Deer Creek _____ 1900
Dexter _____ 1910
Dilley _____ 1900
Dixie (See Rickreal) ___ 1852
Donna _____ 1915
Dorena _____ 1918
Drain _____ 1878
Dufur _____ 1892
Dusty _____ 1900

Eagle Creek _____ 1891
East Portland _____ 1887
East Eugene (See Fair-
  mount) _____ 1909
Echo _____ 1899
Eightmile _____ 1891
Elgin _____ 1898
Elkton _____ 1876
Elmira _____ 1896
Enterprise _____ 1893
Eola _____ 1863
Estacada _____ 1911
Eugene First _____ 1862
Evans _____ 1912

Falls City _____ 1892

Fairmount (See East
Eugene) ------------- 1909
Fairview --------------- 1882
Farmington ------------ 1863
Fern Ridge (See Alva-
dore) ----------------- 1898
Fernvale --------------- 1923
Fir Grove -------------- 1891
Flora ------------------ 1909
Forest Grove ---------- 1883
Fort Rock -------------- 1914
Fossil ----------------- 1911
Franklin --------------- 1897

Gales Creek ------------ 1893
Garibaldi -------------- 1923
Gaston ----------------- 1883
George Hall ------------ 1891
Gladstone -------------- 1908
Glenada ---------------- 1899
Glendale --------------- 1924
Glide ------------------ 1927
Gold Hill -------------- 1891
Gooseberry ------------- 1908
Grande Ronde ---------- 1921
Grants Pass ------------ 1888
Grass Valley ----------- 1906
Grizzley --------------- 1908

Hadleyville ------------ 1891
Halfway ---------------- 1890
Halsey ----------------- 1874
Harris Bridge ---------- 1863
Harrisburg ------------- 1863
Haycreek --------------- 1900
Haystack --------------- 1900
Hebron ----------------- 1861
Hedrix ----------------- 1883
Helix ------------------ 1881
Heppner ---------------- 1893
Herman ----------------- 1900
Hillsboro (Hillsborough)- 1853
Hood River ------------- 1893
Hood River Valley ----- 1884
Holdman ---------------- 1913
Holly ------------------ 1887
Howells Prairie -------- 1847

Independence ---------- 1875
Ione ------------------- 1906

Irrigon ---------------- 1906
Irving ----------------- 1893
Ivison ----------------- 1901

Jasper ----------------- 1891
Jefferson -------------- 1911
Joseph ----------------- 1924
Junction City ---------- 1881

Kellogg ---------------- 1914
Kent ------------------- 1913
Kingston --------------- 1898
Klamath Falls ---------- 1909

Lafayette ---------- 1855
La Grande ------------- 1890
Laidlaw ---------------- 1909
Lakeview --------------- 1900
La Monta --------------- 1909
Lancaster -------------- 1893
Latham ----------------- 1914
Leaburg ---------------- 1891
Lebanon ---------------- 1899
Lexington -------------- 1915
Liberty ---------------- 1882
Liberty Schoolhouse ---- 1913
Looking Glass Prairie -- 1855
Long Tom --------------- 1891
Lorane ----------------- 1891
Lostine ---------------- 1899
Lost Valley ------------ 1891
Lower Cove ------------- 1911
Luckimute -------------- 1848
Lyonsville ------------- 1899

Mabel ------------------ 1891
Madras ----------------- 1906
Marcola ---------------- 1907
Marshfield ------------- 1905
Maupin ----------------- 1916
McGlynn ---------------- 1928
McKay ------------------ 1908
McMinnville ------------ 1855
Medford ---------------- 1884
Mehama ----------------- 1925
Mill City -------------- 1891
Milton ----------------- 1886
Molalla ---------------- 1891
Monitor ---------------- 1891

Monmouth _____ 1856
Monroe _____ 1891
Mosier _____ 1899
Mt. Pleasant _____ 1883
Myrtle Creek _____ 1855
Myrtle Point _____ 1902

Nashville _____ 1901
Newberg _____ 1893
New Bridge _____ 1899
Newport _____ 1924
New Pine Creek _____ 1900
Noble _____ 1899
North Bend _____ 1914
North Plains _____ 1923
North Santiam _____ 1903
North Yamhill (See Yam-
  hill) _____ 1877

Oak Creek _____ 1883
Oak Hill _____ 1900
Oakland _____ 1891
Odell _____ 1906
Ontario _____ 1911
Oregon City _____ 1893
Oretown _____ 1883
Orleans _____ 1923

Parkersville _____ 1899
Pendleton _____ 1891
Perrydale _____ 1887
Phoenix _____ 1906
Pilot Rock _____ 1899
Pine City _____ 1927
Pioneer _____ 1895
Pleasant Hill _____ 1850
Pleasant Valley _____ 1900
Pocahontas _____ 1911
Point Terrace _____ 1891
Portland Central _____ 1903
Portland East Side _____ 1915
Portland Englewood ____ 1922
Portland First _____ 1879
Portland Kern Park ____ 1907
Portland Mallory Ave. __ 1920
Portland Montavilla ____ 1911
Portland R o d n e y Ave.
  (Third) _____ 1893

Portland Rosepark _____ 1925
Portland Ruby Park ____ 1927
Portland Sellwood (See
  Spokane Avenue) _____ 1905
Portland Spokane Avenue 1905
Portland St. Johns ____ 1906
Portland Third (Rodney
  Ave.) _____ 1893
Portland Vernon _____ 1913
Portland Woodlawn ____ 1895
Post _____ 1911
Powers _____ 1926
Prineville _____ 1888
Promise _____ 1908

Rainier _____ 1857
Redmond _____ 1915
Richland _____ 1895
Rickreal (See Dixie) ___ 1848
Riddle _____ 1902
Riverton _____ 1901
Riverview _____ 1911
Rock Point _____ 1901
Roland _____ 1851
Roseburg _____ 1889
Rufus _____ 1913
Rychman _____ 1913

Salem Court _____ 1914
Salem First _____ 1858
Salt Creek _____ 1863
Sand Ridge _____ 1891
Santa Clara _____ 1905
Scio _____ 1859
Scotts Mills _____ 1896
Seaside _____ 1925
Shaddon Schoolhouse ____ 1853
Sheridan _____ 1852
Shoestring Valley _____ 1900
Silver Creek _____ 1857
Silverton _____ 1887
Silverton Hills _____ 1909
South Fork _____ 1854
South Springs _____ 1891
South Yamhill _____ 1858
Spray _____ 1911
Springfield _____ 1882
Spring Valley _____ 1855

Star _____ 1900
Stayton _____ 1881
St. Helens _____ 1883
Strawberry _____ 1908
Svenson _____ 1927
Sweet Home _____ 1916
Sycamore _____ 1891

Talent _____ 1911
The Dalles _____ 1892
Thurston _____ 1890
Tillamook _____ 1892
Trent _____ 1882
Turner _____ 1900

Union _____ 1895
Union Hill _____ 1891
Upper Muddy _____ 1863

Vale _____ 1908
Vernonia _____ 1923

Wallace Butte _____ 1854
Willamina _____ 1910
Wallowa _____ 1907
Walterville _____ 1893
Walton _____ 1891
Wamic _____ 1908
Warrenton _____ 1927
Wasco _____ 1889
Wilbur _____ 1912
Williams _____ 1893
Winchester _____ 1856
Woodburn _____ 1901

"Yamhill, On the Banks
   of" _____ 1846
Yamhill (See North Yam-
   hill) _____ 1877
Yoncalla _____ 1899

CHAPTER VIII
EDUCATIONAL INTERESTS

Disciples of Christ, from the first, have been sympathetic with an educated ministry. Alexander Campbell, who led them out of the wilderness of sectarianism, was a highly educated man, and one of his first steps in propagating the "plea" was the establishment of Bethany College in West Virginia. It was a logical result of his plea for a restoration of primitive Christianity, for Jesus *taught* and *trained* his disciples before sending them out. It may be said, therefore, that this Restoration Movement was born and nourished in an educational atmosphere.

Wherever Disciples of Christ have planted the cause they have sought to perpetuate it by adequate educational institutions which would not only train men to preach the gospel, but would train the rank and file of the people in the proper methods of Bible study. Their educational ideal has been the same as that of John Knox—to give the Bible to the people that they might read it for themselves and not be wholly dependent upon a ministry for their understanding of it. Couple with this a trained ministry and the Word of God can go with eagle wings.

Within a decade of the planting of the first Church of Christ in the state of Oregon active plans were on foot for founding a college. These pioneers in education were destined to suffer many disappointments before their hopes were fully realized, but they were brave souls launching an enterprise on an uncharted sea, and they sailed by the compass of divine love. Some barks were wrecked upon the rocks of disaster, but those captains of Christian education built anew. Perseverance has finally wrought a success in one of the finest educational institutions among Disciples of Christ.

The first move toward a college seems to have been made in the early '50s at Pleasant Hill. However, it never materialized into anything actual. We have not even been able to find the names of the promoters, but one reading the chapters dealing with that period cannot long remain in doubt as to their identity. It is safe to say that there was not a preacher of that day, nor an interested layman, who was not actively concerned in it. Though it never materialized into classic walls and halls, though it never boasted a faculty, though it never bore fruitage through a curriculum, though it is not perpetuated by an honored alumni, yet who can doubt but that the project in contemplation had something to do in making still hotter the educational fires and gave some inspiration for realization at a later day. Pioneers of a movement rarely ever eat the fruits thereof. One man sows, another waters, but it is God who gives the increase.

Another attempt, for which we cannot find the exact beginning date, we list second—at McMinnville. Here an actual organization was made some time in the early '50s. W. T. Newby, Squire Dawson, Sebastian Adams, and James R. McBride were the honored founders thereof. Newby gave 15 acres of ground for its location. The effort was greater than could be successfully handled in those days and soon a debt of $4,000 drove the institution into bankruptcy. The promoters deeded the property to the Baptists in 1857 in consideration of the assumption of the debts. The Baptists have handled it successfully and it now stands as one of the recognized institutions of higher learning under the name of Linfield College.

The next definite step toward a Christian College was at Bethel in 1855. Glen O. Burnett and his wife deeded to the school, under the name of Bethel Institute, 101 acres of land. This was done on May 10, 1856. On the same date Amos Harvey and wife deeded 160 acres of land to the same institution. The school had been actually organized the year before. School sessions continued until some time in the '60s. But long after it ceased to be a religious educational institution the corporation continued to operate its endowment in the interest of the school district in which it was situated, near the foothills east of McCoy. I. N. Mulkey was, perhaps, the last survivor of those who were actively interested in it.

The most pretentious effort toward the establishment of a school in early days was at Monmouth. The news of the Oregon country had gone to the middle states with much promise. John E. Murphey, Elijah Davidson, J. B. Smith, T. H. Lucas, Ira F. Butler, and J. Henry Rountree left Monmouth, Illinois, for the express purpose of establishing a Christian school in Oregon. Upon their arrival they took donation land claims on, and around, the present site of the town of Monmouth. On April 13, 1852, the first steps toward the organization of a school were taken. In 1854 Murphy, Davidson, Smith, Lucas, and S. S. Whitman gave 640 acres of land for a school site. A town was platted and lots were sold. It was named Monmouth after their old home in Illinois. In 1856 a grammar school was built, and J. W. Cowls became the first teacher. In 1858 a house was built costing $5,000, which was known as Monmouth University. This building served as both

church and schoolhouse for a time. In 1871 a brick building was erected which is now the central wing of the
present structure. The bricks were made by the students
on the school grounds, and the cost of the structure was
$16,000. T. F. Campbell (father of Prince L. Campbell,
a president of the University of Oregon for many years)
was the first president, serving from 1869 to 1882.
The name of the institution was afterwards changed
to Christian University. Tuition was made free to
preachers or students for the ministry. D. T. Stanley
became president in 1882 and continued until 1890, during
which time the south wing was built at a cost of $15,000.
The promoters were unable to finance the needs of the
growing institution and in 1892 it was turned over to the
state of Oregon for use as a Normal School. As such it is
used to this day and has the honor of being known as one
of the leading Normal Schools on the Pacific Coast.

These efforts toward a higher education and the training of a Christian ministry were not failures, even though
the institutions started did finally pass out from the control of Disciples of Christ. Ground must be plowed, har-
rowed, and seeded before a crop is reaped. Sometimes it
must be reseeded. These early efforts were but the breaking of the sod, the mellowing of the soil, the planting of
the seed. They paved the way for the final effort which
was destined to become one of the outstanding educational
institutions in the brotherhood.

E. C. Sanderson, upon his graduation from Drake University, had listened to the voice of Horace Greeley in his
famous admonition to young men, "Go west, young man,
go west." Coming to the state of Washington he evangelized for a season, then hearkened to the call of the city

and came to Portland as pastor of the First Church. But God's work for him in the kingdom was neither in evangelism nor in the pastorate. During all this time he felt the urge to educate young men for the ministry. After careful investigation for the best place to begin he decided that Eugene was the logical place. His plan was to establish a Bible College across the street from the campus of the University of Oregon, thus taking advantage of the classical and scientific courses offered by the state in connection with the Bible work of a Christian school. He reasoned that it would lessen the required number of teachers for the Bible School, also the necessary equipment would be reduced to a minimum, thus lessening the expense of operation. It would also be a distinct advantage to the graduates of the Bible College to graduate also from the State University, a recognized school. In July 1895 he moved to Eugene and made preparations for opening such a school. October 6, 1895, school was actually opened in a rented building with five students. Two more students enrolled during that first year. On November 15, 1895, the school was incorporated under the name of Eugene Divinity School. The next year property was purchased immediately across the campus from the State University, and a building erected thereon at a cost of $5,000. This building still stands and is known as Rehm Hall and Cowls Memorial Chapel in memory of the principal donors of the structure. The second building erected was the President's residence, in 1901. In 1908 a new building, constructed entirely of stone, was erected and named the Administration Building. This cost about $40,000, and was dedicated on October 18, 1908. The growth of the student body has been phenomenal and the buildings were soon crowded beyond their capacity for best work. Accordingly two new buildings were erected and dedicated in May, 1921—the Fine Arts Building and the Klinger Gymnasium. The chapel and music department are housed in the former.

The school was incorporated first under the name of Eugene Divinity School. This name did not seem apt to the growing conditions. It began to be more than a mere "school," and its curricula began to incorporate more than "divinity" matters. Accordingly, on May 7, 1908, the Articles of Incorporation were amended by changing the name to Eugene Bible University.

One of the large assets of the school is its library. Adequate provision was made in the erection of the Administration Building for housing this important department. More than 8,000 volumes have been gathered by donation and purchase so the students are adequately equipped for reference purposes. One of the unique features of the library is the collection of rare Bibles. President Sanderson has gathered a large collection of these ancient volumes at great expense.

Meeting the call for a school for young girls who needed a Christian environment the Girls' Junior College was established in 1912. Separate campus and buildings are provided for this department 16 blocks south of the main buildings. The campus contains 15 acres.

Connected with the main school is a department of music and a department of oratory. The primal purpose of these departments is to equip singers for the gospel ministry and young preachers for an acceptable delivery of the gospel message. The orators from the Bible University have many times taken first place in state oratorical contests.

Two instructors deserve special mention herein because they gave up their lives in the work of the school. Ernest C. Wigmore was the instructor in Hebrew from the early days of the school until his death in 1916. David C. Kellems was the head of the Department of Oratory from near the beginning until his untimely death on January 3, 1923. Both men were exceptionally strong characters and have left their impress very markedly upon many of the students. They were loved by all who knew them and enjoyed the confidence of the brotherhood within the state.

The school has grown steadily from the first, each year showing an increase over the year before. The registration for the past year (closing June 1928) was 419.

President Sanderson has been a man of far vision. He has not been content to build a one idea institution. In the fulfillment of this ambition he was instrumental in organizing and incorporating the International Bible Mission on July 12, 1923. While not a part of the legal entity of the Bible University their souls are very largely the same. An extension department of the Bible University was established in Seattle, Washington, on April 24, 1919. On January 25, 1924, the college and church property of the insolvent Christian Missionary and Christian Americanization Movement in Minneapolis, Minnesota, were purchased, and the work was continued there. On March 16, 1924, a new departure for a Christian College, yet withal a laudable enterprise, was undertaken in the establishment of a Christian Hospital, the first among Disciples of Christ on the Pacific coast. A few months later the whole state was electrified with the news that the Mercy Hospital (Catholic) in Eugene had been purchased and added to the equipment of the Pacific Christian Hospital. A school for boys has been opened in California. An extension department of the school has been opened in Manhattan, Kansas, and one at Fort Collins, Colorado. A home for Boys was built in Turner, Oregon.

Among the alumni of the school are some of the notable figures among Churches of Christ. To the present date (1928) the following persons have the privilege, and honor, of calling Eugene Bible University their "Alma Mater." Their names are listed according to the first year of graduation.

1900

Daisley, Marguerite A. (Mrs. E. F. Beaudreau), B.S.L.
Humbert, G. S. O., B.D.

1901

Beaudreau, Edwin F., B.D.
Benton, Harry, B.S.L.; B.O., 1901; B.A., 1928.
Copple, Robert A., B.S.L.
Daisley, Mary A. (Mrs. Harry Benton), B.S.L.; B.O.; B.A., 1924.
Esson, Mrs. Clara G., B.S.L.
Handsaker, John J., B.S.L.

1902

Billington, Frank E., B.D.
Hansaker, C o n s t a n c e (Mrs. Elmer), B.O.
Hoven, Victor E., B.D.; B.O., 1906; D.D., 1921.
Kellems, David Clinton, B.A.; B.D., 1905; D.D., 1915.
Patterson, Elmer Merton, B.D., B.A., 1916; D.D., 1926.
Smith, Alice M. (Mrs. J. J. Handsaker), B.S.L.

1903

Moon, Everard, B.O.; B.A., 1906; B.D., 1918; D.D., 1924.
Read, Ora E. (Mrs. W. A. Hemenway), B.O.

1904

Adkins, Clyde Warrette (Mrs. Mills), B.O.
Green, Cora Ann, B.D.
Green, Leon D., B.D.
Mulkey, Sadie Ensley, B.O.
Woodley, John P., B.S.L.

1905

Denton, Hiram Allen, B.D.; D.D., 1915.
Mahon, Mamie Dorman, B.O.
M a t l o c k, William Theodore. B.S.L.

1906

Horn, Marion F., B.D., B.O.
Linn, Ancil Fillmore, B.S.L.
Lobdell, George L., B.D.
Thompson, M. J., B.S.L.
Ware, Francis A., B.S.L.

1907

Berg, Carl, B.S.L.
Brooke, Frederick M., B.A.; B.D., 1909.
Humbert, Ella M., B.S.L.
Kellems, Louisa Flint, B.O.; M.A., 1927.
Whipple, George Roach, B.S.L.; B.A., 1917.

1908

Beach, Nathan Earl, B.S.L.
Ghormley, J. F., D.D.
Harden, Anna, B.S.L.
Olson, David E., B.A., B.O.; B.D., 1909.
Wigmore, Ernest C., B.A.

1909

Champie, Henry S., B.A.
Curtis, Charles C., B.A.
Curtis, Ethel C., B.S.L.
Elkins, Willard A., B.S.L.
Moore, Charles R., B.A., B.O.; B.D., 1910.
Morgan, Delbert Loyd, B.A.; B.O.
Orrick, John M., B.A.
Stivers, Elijah V., B.A.; B.D., 1916; D.D., 1919.
Tong, Lee, B.S.L.

1910

Childers, S. Earl, B.A.; B.O., 1911; B.D., 1911.
Hickethier, Mamie L. (Mrs. J. E. Yoakum), B.S.L.
Hovis, Victor M., B.A.
Myers, Leon Leroy, B.A.; B.D., 1913; D.D., 1926.
Norcross, David E., B.A.
S h e l l e y, Merle M. (Mrs. Mighton), B.S.L.

1911

Bailey, Mrs. Anna, B.O.
Callison, Walter, B.A.

Chaffee, Lizzie (Mrs. Vaughn), B.S.L.
Dunn, Roy L., B.S.L.
Gressman, William A., B.A.
Hervey, A. Earl, B.S.L.
McConnell, Howard, B.A.; B.O.
Morgan, George W., B.S.L.
Ross, Floyd A., B.A.
Stephens, F. Claude, B.A.
Van Winkle, Henry A., B.A.; B.O.; B.D., 1920; D.D., 1924.
Wilkinson, Mary O. (Mrs. Mary Gervais), B.S.L.; B.O., 1928.
Williams, Nelson O., B.A.

1912

Kellems, Jesse Randolph, B.O.; B.A., 1914; B.D., 1919; D.D., 1919.
Leggett, John Franklin, B.A.; B.D., 1914.
Obert, Leslie, B.S.L.; B.O., 1913.
Ramsey, George H., B.A.; B.D., 1926.
Ray, Ethel Eads, B.A.

1913

Cox, Mary E., B.S.L.
Dodd, Irene F., B.S.L.
Germain, Charles De., B.S.L.
Moon, Rupert Axley, B.A.; B.O.
Sadler, Lee, B.S.L.; B.O.
Wilke, Anna M., B.O.
Y o u n g, G r a c e N., Vocal Teacher's Certificate.

1914

Baker, Anthony Detliffe, B.S.L.
Gilfilen, Goldie Ernestine (Mrs. Everett Persons), Evangelistic Singer's Certificate.
Gilfilen, Silvia Alberta (Mrs. Glen Hutton), Evangelistic Singer's Certificate; B.M., 1922; B.A., 1925.
Hatley, Lusetta Belle (Mrs. Wayne Gilfilen), Evangelistic Singer's Certificate.

Hatley, Loretta Bernice (Mrs. M. A. McQuary), Evangelistic Singer's Certificate.
Lane, Edward Erie, B.S.L.
Mahaffey, Carroll Ghent, B.S.L.
McCallum, Effie Belle, B.D.
R e y n o l d s, Clarence Wallace, B.A.; B.D., 1926.

1915

Ames, Ora Ellsworth, B.A.
Bennett, Abraham Franklin, B.S.L.
Brunk, Hugh D., B.A.; B.D., 1918.
Crabb, William Wheeler, B.S.L.
Curtis, Oliver Langdon, B.S.L.
Fagan, Malcolm Howard, B.A.
Hartley, Albert Charles, B.A.; B.D., 1918.
Humbert, Harold F., B.A.
Kellems, Vera Edwards, B.A.
McHatton, Charles Grandison, B.S.L.
Myers, Walter Lee, B.A.; B.D., 1918.
Putnam, Ralph Lloyd, B.A.

1916

Ames, Ora Ellsworth, B.A.
Bloyd, Hylah Nancy (Mrs. H. J. Berrian), Normal Bible Course.
Fleischman, Earl Emery, B.A.
Hayes, Willard L., B.A.
Williams, Otho H., B.A.
Whipple, Maude Estella, B.A.

1917

Bennett, Vida T., Piano Soloist's Diploma.
Drake, Charles Robert, B.O.; B.A,. 1918.
Ghormley, J. Carlos, B.A.
Healy, Roy L., B.S.L.
Johnstone, Myrtle Fay, B.A.
Johnstone, William James, B.A.
Leggett, Fannie, Normal Bible Course; B.S.L., 1924.

Lutgen, Elma Alice, Piano Teacher's Certificate; Piano Soloist's Diploma, 1918.
McCallum, James Henry, B.A.
Thurston, Clyde Clinton, B.A.; B.D., 1920.
Tupper, Andrew Cecil, B.A.
Turner, William Franklin, D.D.
Vernon, Joyce (Mrs. C. R. Drake), Piano Soloist's Diploma
Wells, Goldie Ruth, B.A.
Whipple, Edna M. (Mrs. Edna Gish), B.A.; B.O.

1918

Atchley, E. F., B.S.L.
Baney, George Wayne, B.A.
Baney, Mary Withycombe, B.A
Bennett, Violet Irene, B.S.L.
Boyd, Joseph David, B.A.; B.D., 1920.
Brunk, Ethel Conneway (Mrs. W. L. Myers), B.A.; Piano Teacher's Certificate, 1922.
Brunk, Velma Lee, B.A.
Clarke, Pearl (Mrs. Carter), Normal Bible Course.
Davis, Bernard S., B.A.
Givens, Walter, B.S.L.
Jenkins, Mabel E. (Mrs. L. H. Benny), B.S.L.
M a d d e n, Maude Whitmore, B.S.L.
Patterson, Emily May, Vocal Soloist's Diploma.
Ritchey, Neva Elvina, B.A.
Smith, Earl M., B.O., B.S.L.
Taylor, May Ethel (Mrs. Henry Reiman), B.S.L.
Williams, Ruth Ellen (Mrs. Carroll C. Roberts), Piano Teacher's Certificate; B.A., 1920.

1919

Benny, Chris John, B.A.
Benny, Ruth Lucille, B.A.
Boyer, Elmer George, B.A.

Burke, Kendall Edward, B.A.
Coley, Fred, B.A.
Douglas, Bertha Colera, B.A.
Drill, Guy L., B.S.L., B.O., 1920.
Drill, Laura L., Normal Bible Course, B.S.L., 1920.
Foust, Jay Simon, B.A.
Harriman, Arthur Absalom, B.A.
Harriman, Fred E., B.A.
Hays, Goldie Taylor, B.S.L.
Hendricks, Kenneth C., B.A.
Hendricks, Grace Paul, B.A.
Leavitt, Linden Gypson, B.S.L.
Leavitt, Teddy Wyatt, B.A.
Louie, Pond Harry, B.A., M.A., 1922.
Mitchell, Hattie Poley, B.A., Evangelistic Singer's Diploma, 1920.
Sheafor, Lucile Elizabeth (Mrs. H. W. Moise), Vocal Soloist's Diploma; Piano Teacher's Diploma, Vocal Teacher's Diploma, 1920; B.S.L., 1921.
Tuttle, Harry A., B.A.
Wakefield, Ethel Harvey, B.A.
Ware, Elizabeth A., B.S.L.

1920

Ashurst, Mary Ethel, Instrumental Teacher's Diploma.
Baird, William Robb, B.A., B.O., B.D., 1923.
Baird, Martha Watson, B.O.
Bower, Milton Ward, B.A., B.D., 1922.
Boyd, Zona Vernon, B.A.
Burke, Edna Lawrence, B.A.
Byerlee, David Allen, B.A.
Dallas, Rex Ruleth, B.A.
Dallas, Marguerite Gebhart, B.S.L.
Dana, Ethel Fay (Mrs. Milton Bower), Instrumental Teacher's Diploma; Piano Soloist's Diploma, 1922; B.A., 1922.
Fishback, Len Bryan, B.A.; B.O., 1922; B.D., 1922.

Gibson, Effie Gladys, B.A.; B.D.; 1921.
Harriman, Dickson Pain, B.A.; Evangelistic Singer's Diploma, 1920.
Harriman, Edna Cornelius, B.S.L.; B.A., 1921; B.O., 1922.
Kirk, Florene (Mrs. C. C. Thurston), B.A.
Newton, Lena Esther, B.A.
Prall, Etta Althea, Normal Bible Course.
Purnell, Frank Lewis, B.A.
Richards, Charles Harold, Evangelistic Singer's Diploma; Vocal Soloist's Diploma; B.M., 1926.
Roberts, Carroll Curtis, B.A.
Rowe, Shirley Irving, B.A.
Stover, Ramona Adelphine (Mrs. N. J. Reasoner), B.A.
Sutton, William Phene, B.A., B.O., 1921.

1921

Applebury, Theodore Ralph, B.A.; B.D., 1923.
Bendshadler, Stella Catherine, Piano Teacher's Certificate; Piano Soloist's Diploma, 1922.
Benny, Louis Henry, B.S.L.; B.O., 1922.
Boyd, Ruth Edith (Mrs. Lorraine Stivers), Piano Soloist's Diploma; B.A., 1923.
Harding, Cecile Elizabeth, Vocal Soloist's Diploma; Piano Teacher's Certificate; Evangelistic Singer's Certificate, 1925; B.M., 1925.
Helseth, Gladys Wells, B.A.
Jones, Lester Irwin, B.A.; B.D., 1923.
Kellems, Vivian, B.O.
Matlock, Gareld Lee, B.A.; B.O., 1922; B.D., 1923.
Miles, Carl S., B.A.

Pointer, James Andrew, B.O.; B.A., 1925.

Pointer, Lucy E., B.S.L.

Pope, Margaret Olive (Mrs. W. P. Sutton), B.S.L.

Purnell, Una Hall, B.A.

Reininger, Loa Jane (Mrs. Eldon L. Wood), Piano Teacher's Certificate; B.A., 1925; B.M., 1926.

Sponsler, John Chester, B.A.

Straub, Walter Lewis, B.S.L.; B.A., 1922; B.D., 1926; B.O., 1928

Udasco, Canuto S., B.A.

Wing, James Orye, B.A.

1922

Applebury, Josephine, B.S.L.

Baker, Kathryn Isabel (Mrs. Wm. V. Barney), B.A.

Bodine, Bess Belle, B.A.

Boyd, Lulu Lois (Mrs. Alvin Braden), Piano Teacher's Certificate; B.A., 1923.

Brunk, Alice Pauline (Mrs. Ross Guiley), B.A.

Carlson, Jessie Baptie, B.A., B.M.

Carlson, John Eric, B.A.; B.O., 1923; B.D., 1923.

Cole, Ruby Ann, B. A.; B.O., 1924.

Farnham, Grace Ella, B.A.

Fishback, Mildred Leone, B.A.

Goodwin, Alonzo Theodore, B.A.

Goodwin, Helen May (Mrs. Hugh McCallum), B.A.

Jones, Wallace Edgar, B.A.

Lamb, Rhoda Enid, B.A.

Lattin, Grant Faith, B.A.

Lattin, Winnie Etta, B.A.

Phillips, Beatrice Grace, Piano Teacher's Certificate.

Phillips, Charles Henry, B.A.

Shaffer, Mrs. Caroline, Piano Teacher's Certificate.

Wood, Eldon Lester, B.A.; B.O.; B.D., 1924.

Wyatt, Erna, Piano Teacher's Certificate; B.S.L., 1923.

1923

Arant, Francis Marion, B.A.; B.D., 1926.

Calvert, Catherine Elizabeth (Mrs. Jim Y. Maxwell), B.S.L.

Goodwin, Miriam Williams, B.A.

Guiley, Ross, B.A.; B.D., 1927.

Guiley, Mary, B.A.

Headrick, Ella Faye (Mrs. Don Rickerson), B.A.

Hohgatt, Cyrus Hersell, B.D.; B.M., 1923; B.O., 1924; D.M., 1926.

Isaacson, Ralph Wesley, B.A.

Jones, Nellie Lorentzen, B.A.; Piano Teacher's Certificate.

McCallum, Hugh Neal, B.A.; B.D., 1925.

Meisinger, George Eugene, B.A.

Mick, Orville F., B.A.; B.D., 1925.

Neely, Grace Emily (Mrs. Tom Hughes) Certificate in Elocution and Oratory.

Phillips, Amy Carson, B.A.

Phillips, Clifton Alroy, B.O.; B.A., 1925.

Piper, William Chauncy, B.A.

Robertson, Donna Elizabeth (Mrs. Donna Cross), Piano Teacher's Certificate.

Schmid, Gottlieb, B.A.

Stevens, Mary E., B.A.

Stivers, Davison Lorraine, B.A.; B.D., 1925; B.O., 1925.

Whisler, Vivian Gwendoline, B.M.

White, Hazel Geneva, B.A.

1924

Aquino, Vicente V., B.A.

Bothwell, Rosella Mae, B.S.L.

Carter, Victor C., B.A.

Chapman, Anna Elizabeth, B.A.; M.A., 1927; Graduate Nurse's Diploma, 1927.

Cooper, Leatha Whisler, B.A.
Dunn, Josephine Mae, B.S.L.;
B.O., 1926; B.A., 1927.
Helseth, Emil, B.A.
Humphreys, Leta M., B.A.
Isaacson, Laverne Sacks, B.A.
Kratz, David Leander, B.A.
Martin, Lewis Cromwell, B.A.
Newman, Emmett Guy, B.O.
Strome, Erma Elsadie, B.A.
Taubman, George P., D.D.

1925

Brownfield, Mildred Irene, B.A.,
B.O., 1927.
Cadaos, Alejandro Pablo y, B.A.
Chamlee, Lonnie Ivy, B.A.
Cochrane, Curtis Maxwell, B.S.L.
Delmendo, Juan, B.A.
Dent, Dorsey Edward, B.A.
Foster, Ransom Hugh, B.S.L.
Gibson, Dorothy May, B.A.
Gilstrap, Mary Edna, Bible
Teacher Training Certificate.
Harding, Mary Cecile, B.A.
Knott, Harold Elkin, B.D.; D.D.,
1927.
Ladd, James Earl, B.A.; B.D.,
1928.
Lord, Laura Blackwell, B.A.
McClendon, Clifton Elizabeth
(Mrs. James Earl Ladd),
B.A.; B.O.
Nankivell, Wilfred Frank, B.M.;
B.A., 1926; B.D., 1927.
Neely, Claude James, Evangel-
istic Singer's Certificate; B.M.,
1927; B.O., 1928.
Nelson, Laura, B.O.
Priest, Donald Dunbar, B.A.
Priest, Nellie Claire, B.A.
Pruitt, Veltie, B.M.
Rice, Ward Adrian, B.A.
Taylor, Ivy Ruby, B.O.

1926

Applegate, Hortense Bennett,
B.A.
Bass, Herbert James, B.A.

Carey, Lucille Meserve, B.A.
Carroll, John Fleming, B.S.L.
Cooper, Oscar A., B.A.; B.D.,
1928.
Cunningham, Lolita Carrie, B.A.
Davis, James E., D.D.
Farrow, Eugene Oregon, B.A.
Fellers, Martha Ella, B.A.
Fite, John Raymond, B.A.
Hale, James Willis, B.A.; B.O.,
1927.
Ivie, Nora E., Piano Teacher's
Certificate.
Jessup, Dorothy Anna, B.A.
Jordan, Galen Elmer, B.A.
Kellems, Hazel Dean, B.A.; B.O.
Master, Edwin Spencer, B.A.
McCallum, James S., D.D.
Mick, Arlouine Johnson, B.A.
Morgan, Clarence Carnes, B.S.L.
Mick, Helen Mae, B.A.
Neely, Helen DeRush, Piano
Teacher's Certificate.
Nelson, Neva Church, B.A.
Reagan, Affie Pauline, B.A.
Scott, Wilma Isabel, B.A.
Searle, Allan Grant, Director of
Evangelistic Singing.
Springer, George W., B.A.
Stansbury, Howard G., B.A.
Toogood, Henry, B.A.
Wells, W. Lawrence, B.A.; B.D.,
1928.

1927

Allen, Ruby Jayne, Graduate
Nurse's Diploma.
Applegate, Joseph Merle, B.A.
Batman, Edna M., Graduate
Nurse's Diploma.
Barney, William Virgil, B.A.
Bennett, Lucille, Graduate
Nurse's Diploma.
Bentley, Gerald Gideon, B.A.
Bingman, Mildred E., Graduate
Nurse's Diploma.
Boulten, Clarence Arthur, B.A.
Carey, Clifford Lawrence, B.A.

Champie, Vera, Piano Teacher's Diploma.

Clark, Worcester A., Evangelistic Singer's Diploma.

Cunningham, John Franklin, B.A.

Dandy, Esther Marguerite, Graduate Nurse's Diploma.

Gordon, Alexander Campbell Duff, B.A.

Harden, Mary, Piano Teacher's Diploma.

Hovrud, Oscar Elmer, B.A.

Hendricks, Russell Gordon, B.A.

Isaacson, Fay Miller, B.A.

Jones, Clara Lillian, Graduate Nurse's Diploma.

Kawaguchi, Sadaichi, B.S.L.

Landles, Andrew, B.M.

Moberg, James Dalgety, B.A.

Nankivell, Dora, Piano Teacher's Diploma.

Nations, Gilbert O., D.D.

Rickerson, Donald Newton, B.A.

Scates, Vida M., Graduate Nurse's Diploma.

Soward, Earl Lavanda, B.A.

Strahm, Gladys Ivista, B.A.

Street, Mary Ruth, B.A.

Staley, Edna E., Graduate Nurse's Diploma.

Sugano, Hiromu, B.A.

Smith, Goldie Iowa, Normal Bible Certificate.

Turner, Matthew John, B.A.

Wilson, Florence Esson, Graduate Nurse's Diploma.

1928

Barnes, Orpha, Graduate Nurse's Diploma.

Bartlett, Laurence Gerald, Evangelistic Song Director's Diploma.

Bates, A. C., B.S.L.

Bright, Annie M., Graduate Nurse's Diploma.

Carter, Neva Faye, Graduate Nurse's Diploma.

Chandler, Jessie Lorena, Evangelistic Song Director's Diploma.

Chase, Helen Wostell, Graduate Nurse's Diploma.

Cram, Mabel Fortune, Graduate Nurse's Diploma.

Downing, Earl F., B.A.

Elliott, Stephen, B.A.

Ellis, Edith M., Graduate Nurse's Diploma.

Estepa, Blas, B.A.

Ferebee, Florence Ingalls, B.A.

Hooton Dorothy May, Graduate Nurse's Diploma.

Jacobson, Alice Margaret, Graduate Nurse's Diploma.

Johnson, Thomas Henry, B.D.

Johnson, George F. G., B.A.

Johnson, Ruth Ellis, B.A.

Miller, Ellen Jane, B.S.L.

Miller, Ethel Carolyn, Graduate Nurse's Diploma.

Mooers, Leland L., B.S.L.

Morgan, James Evan, B.A.

Mullins, Hazel, Graduate Nurse's Diploma.

Nutting, David Walton, B.D.

Peterson, Mary Elizabeth, B.O.

Peterson, Orval Douglas, B.A.

Powers, Gwen Stivers, B.M.

Respess, Roy Earl, B.A.

Ross, George Alan, B.A.

Sloan, Errol Berry, B.A.

Stram, Walter Ernest, B.A.

Swander, Clarence F., M.A.

Trowbridge, Verda V., Graduate Nurse's Diploma.

Vail, John Lester, B.A.

Degrees granted for which no dates are available:

Burton, B. B., D.D.

Rose, Morton L., D.D.

Smith, Harry D., D.D.

Weimer, George, D.D.

CHAPTER IX

JOURNALISM

Disciples of Christ have always been a reading people. That accounts for their being an informed people. In the beginning days every man carried his New Testament as zealously as a cowboy toted his pistol on the range. He was as familiar with it, too. Alexander Campbell, from the beginning of the Restoration Movement, spread his propaganda through the medium of the printed page. The *Christian Baptist* and the *Millennial Harbinger* were household companions among disciples in an early day. The *Christian Standard* and *The Christian-Evangelist* were their successors in the general field of Christian journalism. Each section of the country, likewise, has tried its hand at publishing papers. The journalistic cemetery is full of deceased periodicals. Most of these local efforts came to grief through lack of financial support. Yet they paved the way for a more permanent and more successful era for the Christian paper.

Oregon disciples have been no exception to the rule. It has been difficult to gather complete information about all the papers published within the state during the life of the Restoration Movement. We are by no means sure that we have a complete record. Exact dates are lacking in many cases, and in other cases we have been able to supply approximate dates only by Sherlock Holmes methods. To the best of our information papers in Oregon have been published as follows:

154

The *Christian Herald* seems to have been the first effort. We have seen a copy that bears the date of June 27, 1888, and is marked Volume XVII, Number 4. Figuring back this would give the initial date of publication as June 6, 1872. This assumes that it was a weekly publication, and makes no allowance for missed copies. However that may be, the year 1872 is fairly accurate. T. F. Campbell, J. F. Floyd, and D. T. Stanley are named as the editors. The place of publication seems to have been Monmouth, though we have no evidence that it continued there throughout the 17 years of its life.

The *Pacific Christian Messenger* was being published in Monmouth in 1880. There is in the state office one sheet from Number 47, published in November of that year. The page bearing the volume number is missing. T. F. Campbell was the editor. This date makes it quite certain that the *Christian Herald,* mentioned above, was not being published at Monmouth at that date. It would seem, too, that T. F. Campbell had some time previously ceased editing the *Christian Herald* and had established the *Pacific Christian Messenger* in its stead. Doubtless the *Christian Herald* was moved elsewhere.

The *Harbinger* was published in Portland in 1892 by D. T. Stanley. There is in the state office a copy bearing the imprint of Volume II, Number 31, dated August 6, 1892. Figuring back from this it would make the initial number of the paper appear about January 8, 1891. Knowing that D. T. Stanley was connected with the *Christian Herald* in 1888 it would seem to be a reasonable inference that he and Campbell separated their newspaper interests, Stanley establishing the *Harbinger* in Portland and Campbell establishing the *Pacific Christian Messenger* in Monmouth. The *Christian Herald* may have bequeathed a legacy to both the other publications. Some time between August 6, 1892 and July 15, 1893 the *Harbinger* was moved to San Francisco. G. K. Berry, of Portland, who was prominent for a number of years in Pacific coast journalism, says:

"While I was preaching in Eureka, California, there was a paper published in San Francisco by Geo. Sweaney, and one in Portland by D. T. Stanley. The two editors had some contention at times . . . . Sweaney's paper was discontinued. The *Harbinger* was taken to San Francisco and the name changed to the *Pacific Christian*."

The *Pacific Christian* was the merger, as stated above, of the *Harbinger* and some other paper published in San Francisco. The *Harbinger* continued for some time after its removal to California. How long we do not know. Some time after the merger W. B. Berry and J. F. Ghormley bought the paper. An office was opened in Portland while the publication continued in San Francisco. Oregon disciples recognized it as jointly an Oregon paper as is shown by the minutes of the convention in 1899. G. K. Berry, a brother to W. B. Berry, finally bought Ghormley's interest in the paper and the two brothers continued to publish it until it was finally sold to the California State Board (North), when it became purely a California paper. It was afterwards purchased by *The Christian-Evangelist*, of St. Louis, and publication ceased entirely.

The *Christian Reporter* was a state paper published by J. B. Lister during his secretaryship, 1894-1903. This was sent out from his office in Eugene and was published purely in the interest of Oregon work.

The *Apostolic Appeal* was launched by the State Board in 1907. At this time there was no medium through which to reach the churches effectively with messages from the state office. After due consideration the State Board decided to publish a paper. The initial number was printed in September 1907, edited by C. F. Swander, then Recording Secretary of the State Board and pastor of the church at McMinnville. It was a monthly publication. It was in the field just five years and ceased then only because of another paper having started in the meantime that was better able to handle the journalistic side of Oregon work than could be done from the state office. The State Board had free access to its columns.

The *Church and School* commenced publication in Eugene during 1909 by the Eugene Bible University, and was edited by Harry Benton. It was the paper that succeeded the *Apostolic Appeal* in 1912. Its name was changed in 1916 to the *Christian Journal,* which made it more comprehensive in character and gave it a wider scope. The name was changed again in 1925 to the *World Evangel,* and is being published under that title today. This paper goes out over the entire Northwest and into much of California.

The *State Missions Bulletin* had its origin in October, 1919. The State Secretary felt the need of a regular communication with the pastors of the state, such as would not properly belong in the columns of a paper circulating in other states. It began by the printing of a news letter on the Multigraph which was set up somewhat after the fashion of a newspaper. This was continued under that policy until the fall of 1925. During this time many others besides preachers had seen the *Bulletin* and had asked for copies to be sent to them. In September 1925 the State Board decided that the *Bulletin* should go to as many people as possible, so a selected list of about 1,500 names was made and it was published bimonthly for a few months. This entailed a vast amount of extra labor on the Secretary and the list grew. In May 1926 the State Board authorized the publication monthly (except the summer months), the printing was turned over to a commercial shop, and an issue of 5,000 was published for distribution among the churches. It is not a newspaper, nor does it pretend to occupy that field. It confines itself solely to State Missions and its problems, educating the people to the needs of the state and inspiring them to larger giving. It has met with a warm reception among the people. The preachers, almost without exception, assist in the distribution of it.

CHAPTER X

WOMAN'S WORK

The history of Disciples of Christ in any state is incomplete without reference to the part women have played in its development. Women have played a large part in Oregon history. The organization of women, known as the Woman's Missionary Society, has been more responsible for the growth of missionary sentiment and knowledge than any other agency in the church. Aside from this they have raised huge sums of money for missionary purposes, they have kept the cause alive in places where otherwise it would have died, and in some instances they have been the forerunner of the church organization.

The Christian Woman's Board of Missions had its origin at the General Convention in Cincinnati, Ohio, in 1874. Oregon had a delegate present at that meeting and a helper in the organization of the new society. Mrs. E. J. Barker, of Albany, had that honor. She returned to Oregon full of enthusiasm for the new movement and preached it in season and out of season. The reception was not as enthusiastic as the presentation. At that time there was considerable prejudice against a woman's society. Did not Paul command women to "keep silence in the church"? Then, too, the evangelistic fever was at white heat and folks didn't have time to think much about missionary problems. Added to that was a prevalent skittishness toward missionary societies. Already Boards existed for work in Home and Foreign fields—why should we duplicate their work with a new society proposing to work in both fields? Why should women organize apart from men anyway? Perhaps the greatest obstacle presented was a friendly indifference. All other objections could be met with argument, and argument buttressed with facts. But it took something more than argument to break down an indifference that was friendly but noncooperative.

But the seed was planted, first in the hearts of individual women, and there were even a few preachers who dared to champion the women's cause. During the early '80s a few auxiliaries (as they were then called) were organized in the state. It was not until 1888 that definite steps were taken toward organizing the state under the tutelage of the National Board. This was accomplished immediately through the visit of W. K. Azbill who had been sent to the state by the National Board. He visited many of the churches, presenting the claims of the C. W. B. M., as it was popularly known, breaking down prejudice, and enlisting helpfulness among women, laymen and preachers. As a culmination of his work a meeting was called in the city of Portland and an organization effected. Mrs. L. R. Osborne, of Salem, was honored with the first presidency of the state society. It was an honor she retained for two years. Mrs. Eugenia Warriner Gillingham, also of Salem, was honored with the first secretaryship. They were both chosen from the same city in order that they might work together directly without more expense than was absolutely necessary. They were organizing for the purpose of spending as much money as possible for missionary purposes and not one penny more for overhead expense than was absolutely necessary.

The earnestness of soul of these women was manifested not alone in organization. A frequent weakness of organized bodies is that all the energy and enthusiasm of the constituent members is spent in organizing so that there is no power for the things it was organized to do. Like Mark Twain's steamboat, whose engine was so small that when it whistled it exhausted all the steam and couldn't run until it got up more steam, so these organizations exhaust themselves just blowing off steam, and then they cannot run until they get up more steam. By the time that comes to pass they have lost their passion for the things they were organized to do. Not so these women of Oregon. They made their organization quietly and simply and immediately set about to work it. A mission point was necessary else there would be no excuse for organizing, and they could not effectively appeal for its extension among the churches unless they had a definite objective. The work was at hand, at their very door, the key to the development of the Restoration Movement through all the state. The First Church of Portland was then a struggling group of Christians only, meeting in a tabernacle behind the barn of Portland's leading citizen. It had had a long, precarious existence. The outlook was not promising. These women did not ask for some easy task, or one where they would be certain to make a shining record at the next convention. But they chose the hardest, most unpromising field in the state. Through this newly organized State Board of women the National Board took Portland First as a mission point and David Wetzel became the missionary pastor. From this time new life came to the discouraged band, fortune has smiled upon them, and today a magnificent temple of worship and a membership of more than 1,200 souls stand as the fruitage of that first effort of Oregon women to organize for missionary work.

The work of this organization has grown from that humble beginning coincident with the birth of the parent society in 1874 until today (1928) there are 76 societies and nearly 2,500 members representing the woman's work in Oregon.

Other churches assisted through this agency in the state have been Rodney Ave. (Portland), Corvallis and Pendleton. These are now strong churches and are a crown of rejoicing to the society that assisted them into a larger life.

One other special task within the state was assumed by this society—the Chinese Mission in Portland. This mission was opened through the ministry of David Wetzel, in 1891, while he was the missionary pastor of the First Church. At the General Convention held at Nashville, Tennessee, that year, the National C. W. B. M. Board appropriated $300 for the Chinese Mission while the First Church pledged a like amount. It was difficult to get competent teachers and the coming year was a struggle. In 1892 Jeu Hawk, a graduate of Drake University, was sent by the National Board to take charge of the Mission. He continued with it until 1900 when he returned to China. Louie Hugh, and his wife Grace, were then placed in charge and they remained until 1909. In 1906 Grace Hugh passed over to the other side and left her husband and children alone. During this administration the Mission reached its apex of Christian usefulness. In 1909 Louie Hugh resigned to accept a government position in China.

His two children were later returned to Portland and were with the Mission until it closed in 1924.

During the administration of Louie Hugh a Chinese lad was in preparation for this work in Eugene Bible University. Upon the resignation of Louie Hugh, Lee Tong stepped into the leadership of the Mission where he continued until 1915. Intimately associated with the Mission throughout all its history to this time was the saintly character, Mrs. A. A. Kellogg. During these years she played the part of fairy godmother to the Mission, teaching, leading, advising, superintending and praying for its success.

Following the removal of Lee Tong to San Francisco the work became more or less demoralized. At times it would flourish and many consecrated lives went into its personnel of teachers and leaders. For a season its management was merged with that of all the Oriental Missions on the coast and a superintendent made periodical visits to oversee it. M. D. Clubb held that position of superintendent. But this did not cause the mission to prosper. The Chinese population of Portland was declining. It seemed, too, that there must be some local management more than could be vested in a faculty of teachers. Finally the management of the Mission was placed in the hands of a Board of six Portland people who acted in an advisory capacity only. This committee was composed of J. F. Faust, Joseph D. Boyd, Mrs. H. L. Ganoe, Mrs. Ward B. Swope, Mrs. A. B. Brown, and C. F. Swander. This committee continued for more than two years and finally recommended that the Mission either be placed upon a basis with a real local head to it, or discontinued. The National

Board felt that the cost of maintaining the Mission was greater than the results coming from it, and on the first of August, 1924, it was formally closed. The Chinese members of the Mission practically all went to other Chinese Missions in town.

Oregon's best womanhood has gone into the work of furthering the interests of missions through the C. W. B. M. The following women have served it as state president since its organization: Mrs. Laura Osborne, 2 years; Mrs. F. H. Stewart, 2 years; Mrs. E. S. Leach, 1 year; Mrs. H. A. Denton, 4 years; Mrs. Albyn Esson, 4 years; Mrs. W. W. Bristow, 1 year; Mrs. Ella Humbert, 10 years; Mrs. F. E. Jones, 1 year; Mrs. E. C. Wigmore, 3 years; Mrs. J. A. Bennett, 2 years; Mrs. Louisa F. Kellems, 2 years; Mrs. W. B. Swope, 1 year; Mrs. M. H. Kendall, 5 years; Mrs. T. J. Bailey, 2 years. This carries up to June 30, 1928.

The following women have served as secretary since the beginning: Mrs. Eugenia F. Gillingham, Miss Nellie Rhodes, Mrs. L. R. Osborne, Mrs. L. F. Stephens, Mrs. J. C. McKern, Mrs. E. C. Sanderson, Mrs. Lulu Burnett, Mrs. M. A. Ghormley, Mrs. Ella Humbert, Mrs. Albyn Esson, Mrs. T. S. Handsaker, Mrs. C. O. Kurtz, Mrs. W. B. Swope, Mrs. Ellen Hunter, Mrs. H. A. Cooley, Mrs. Barton Z. Riggs, Mrs. W. A. Reid. This carries up to June 30, 1928.

The growth in membership and funds of the Oregon Women's Work has been remarkable and fully justifies the movement. We give it here year by year, for the year closing June 30.

Year	Membership	Money	Year	Membership	Money
1888		$ 25.00	1908-09	1,010	$2,292.21
1888-89	55	91.93	1909-10	1,401	2,824.77
1889-90	180	326.82	1910-11	1,397	3,308.17
1890-91	100	276.65	1911-12	1,600	3,824.69
1891-92	190	244.27	1912-13	1,691	3,493.87
1892-93	717	617.80	1913-14	1,810	4,059.85
1893-94	600	624.99	1914-15	1,623	3,946.31
1894-95	528	483.33	1915-16	1,627	3,593.43
1895-96	447	600.01	1916-17	1,428	3,959.96
1896-97	447	362.46	1917-18	1,632	4,179.71
1897-98	285	434.58	1918-19	1,492	3,937.34
1898-99	272	405.00	1919-20	1,676	4,472.01
1899-00	357	676.97	1920-21	1,760	15,241.11
1900-01	408	717.86	1921-22	1,886	4,644.15
1901-02	497	746.66	1922-23	1,971	4,698.44
1902-03	471	674.08	1923-24	2,304	8,644.94
1903-04	471	644.11	1924-25	2,265	5,567.32
1904-05	493	806.21	1925-26	2,730	5,978.89
1905-06	616	969.32	1926-27	2,496	6,694.46
1906-07	615	1,456.78	1927-28	2,452	7,118.92
1907-08	858	2,131.03			

Of the more than $15,000 raised in 1920-21, $10,000 was from the Keyt estate, Perrydale, Oregon. The amount was raised to the figure it was in 1923-24 through the Golden Jubilee campaign.

CHAPTER XI

THE BIBLE SCHOOLS

No people have been more zealous in propagating Bible School work than Disciples of Christ. It is impossible to determine when and where the first Bible School among us was organized in Oregon. Doubtless it was some time after churches began to be organized. Doubtless, too, the first Sunday Schools were crude affairs compared to present day organizations. They could be nothing else in small, one room buildings.

The earliest printed records of our conventions date back to 1880. At a meeting of the Annual State Cooperation held in Portland on November 10, 1880, the program contained the subject of Sunday Schools for discussion. A paragraph from that record is interesting:

"The discussion of this subject (Sunday Schools) manifested a great anxiety on the part of all to see a more general interest in this part of the church work. Members thought that the way to build up a church was to organize and maintain a live Sunday School. The fact that the young and rising generation need special moral restraints was a great argument for implanting the young mind with heart truths, religious, Christian truths which will make an impression in youth which cannot be made at any other time in life. The Sunday School belongs to the church and not the church to the school, nor yet the school to the world. Therefore ought the church to appoint all the officers and teachers and the older members most especially to attend and lend their assistance. One said that his observation taught him that in the Sunday Schools he had visited lately, the secret of the successful schools was the attendance and supervision of the older members of the church."

We have heard some of these same thoughts presented in recent years by Sunday School workers as being modern discoveries. A wise man said once that there is nothing new under the sun.

In the 1882 convention at Eugene the same subject was again discussed under the title, "Relation of the Sunday School to the Church," by R. G. Callison. There is nothing to indicate, however, that Sunday Schools had any greater inning in the convention than as a theme for discussion. It was not until 1891 that steps were taken to organize the Sunday Schools of the State for more effective service. At the convention that year a "Sunday School Day" was designated on the program, Monday, June 22. It is appropriate that the minutes of that meeting should be reproduced here. They are as follows:

SUNDAY SCHOOL DAY

Monday, June 22

9:30 A.M. Song service led by P. R. Burnett.

P. R. Burnett was elected chairman.

10 A.M. W. R. Williams proposed that the Sunday School work be discussed, and plans adopted for the future year, and with earnestness spoke of the benefits of Sunday School work. Remarks were made by J. J. Moss, T. F. Brown, A. B. Wade, and others.

It was moved that a State Sunday School Association be formed and after enthusiastic discussion, the motion was adopted.

The following officers were elected for the coming year:

W. R. Williams, Salem, President.

Mrs. Laura Osborne, Salem, Secretary.

H. A. Johnson, Salem, Treasurer.

It was moved that W. R. Williams conduct a model Sunday School the coming Sunday. The motion was adopted.

It was further adopted that the officers of the Association arrange a program for the forenoon of the first Sunday of our next Annual Meeting.

It was further ordered that one day of our Annual Meeting be given to the Sunday School Association; program to be furnished by the officers of the Association.

No program being prepared for this preliminary meeting, the balance of the day was taken up by social services and preaching.

LAURA OSBORNE, Secretary.   W. R. WILLIAMS, President.

The minutes of the next Lord's Day simply carry the announcement that "Sunday School was conducted by W. R. Williams." It does not say whether or not it was a "model" school.

A good deal of objection to organized Sunday School work must have been manifested at that meeting. It is said that when the question of organizing was considered "all the preachers in the convention, except Peter Burnett, left the tabernacle." When God's hour is ready to strike even preachers cannot hold silent the gong! The Association was launched without preachers (note the plural; it had one preacher in it) and has had a continuous existence since.

The history of organized Sunday School work in Oregon revolves most largely around the personality and activities of Mrs. Clara G. Esson. She was elected president of the Association in 1898 and, with the exception of one year on account of illness, she continued in that position until 1908. She was then "recalled" from the presidency for the purpose of advancing her to a larger field of usefulness —the superintendency. She still continues to hold that position under the title of State Bible School Superintendent. She will this year (1928) round out 20 years of service in that capacity. A large portion of the time she has done the work under the handicap of poor health, but she has done the work. Her spirit has never flagged. She has worked in season and out of season. Upon more than one occasion her brethren have shown their love in a material way. During a long illness with smallpox they sent her special offerings to an amount that about cared for the expenses of her illness. In 1926 her friends raised a purse which amounted to more than $100, with which

they purchased her a fine gold watch and gave her the
balance in cash. There is no person in the state whom
the people delight to honor more than their beloved Bible
School leader.

Other people who have served in the State Sunday School
work in an official capacity are as follows: W. H. Osborne,
President in 1892; S. D. Read, President in 1893 and 1894;
W. H. Hawley, President 1895-97; E. M. Patterson, President in 1901; H. C. Epley, President 1908-1916. At the
1916 convention the Bible School work was correlated with
the State Board as a department thereof, the State Superintendent was constituted a member of the State Board, and
a President of Sunday School work was no longer elected.

At the convention in 1896 W. H. Hawley, then President, made a recommendation that Rally Day each year be
made the time for an offering for State Bible School work.
In the beginning days the funds for carrying on the work
were scarce and spasmodic. Rather weakly at first did the
Rally Day idea work. But gradually the schools began to
take hold of it, until now it is considered the orthodox
thing to take an offering for State Bible School work on
Rally Day. When Mrs. Esson first took up the field work
it was on the understanding that the outgo should not exceed the income. In those beginning days her "outgoing"
was sometimes seriously handicapped, and only she and
the good Lord will probably ever know just how she kept
from running a deficit. Some folks who were near to the
work have their suspicions. But it is to the credit of Mrs.
Esson and her work that the Bible School department has
always been self-sustaining. After the amalgamation of
the Bible School work with the State Board the Board
guaranteed her a definite salary and expenses—if the in-

come of the Department did not meet this the General Fund would do so. Again to her credit it must be recorded that the State Board has never been called upon to make good the guarantee except to advance money for a short time during a period of lean collections.

The 1896 convention witnessed another incident that was unique. J. W. Jenkins, pastor at Hood River, brought to the convention five nickels from five little girls in his congregation. This presentation moved the convention to pass a resolution that "we each bring five cents when we come to convention next year to be used in State Sunday School work." The enthusiasm of the incident occasioned an amendment to the resolution to the effect that "we begin it NOW." The hat was passed and $4.05 was returned, which would indicate either that there were only 81 present in that meeting, or that some found it easier to vote than to pay. This fund was named the "Little Girls' Fund."

The convention of 1904 decided upon a great forward move. It was decided to employ a field worker. For many years this idea had been incubating in the minds of Sunday School leaders, but never before had they felt the courage to attempt it. After careful investigation and preparation J. P. Conder was called from West Virginia and he came to Oregon in time for the 1905 convention. He was to receive a salary of $1,000 per year and necessary expenses, the Sunday School Board to stand responsible for $500 of it and he to raise the balance in the field. He served only one year, but the record says he did a good work.

The field was without a man for the following year. In October of 1907 E. R. Moon assumed the task and con-

tinued faithfully in it for about nine months. There was
no other field worker then until Mrs. Esson took it up in
February 1909.

At the 1913 convention much interest was aroused by a
class of boys walking to Turner from Tillamook, with their
pastor, R. E. Jope.

One of the most outstanding things accomplished by the
State Bible School work is the conducting of a Leadership
Training School at the state convention, meeting the International standard in the course given. This was first
demonstrated in the 1922 convention and has been a
regular feature since that time.

CHAPTER XII

CHRISTIAN ENDEAVOR

Very little of historic importance is discoverable about the work of Christian Endeavor in Oregon. Since that society did not come into existence until 1881, and that upon the Atlantic coast, it is not to be expected that a very early presence of it on the Pacific coast should be found. The first mention of the representation of Christian Endeavor in the state conventions is in the report of 1893. A constitution of the state society is recorded in these minutes.

In the report for 1899 there are revealed 58 societies, with a membership of 982, and $90.40 was raised for all purposes through the state society.

The 1900 convention was enthusiastic in attendance— 103 delegates in attendance. They voted that year for each society to pay one dollar for state work.

Christian Endeavor in Oregon has revolved about the personalities of three leaders more than aught else. G. Evert Baker, of Portland, was state President for a considerable time, and under his leadership the work got in good swing. Mrs. Mary D. Benton, of Eugene came to the presidency under the handicap of an indebtedness which she felt the moral obligation of paying. It is to her credit that this was discharged, but it was done through her zeal and enthusiasm. After the debt was paid she led the Endeavorers out into a more loyal support of the state work. Walter L. Myers has been the state Superintendent of Christian Endeavor ever since the Endeavor work has been amalgamated with the State Board as a department thereof. He has a large influence with the young people, not only of Churches of Christ, but in the Union movement.

Formerly Christian Endeavor Day at Turner fell on Friday; but by mutual consent the Endeavorers exchanged Friday for Saturday with the college interests. It was deemed a better arrangement for the Endeavor program in that it was thought more young people could attend on Saturday than any other day of the week.

An annual feature of the Endeavor Day at Turner is the bonfire. An effort is made to have a huge pile of combustibles ready for ignition as soon as the evening program is finished in the tabernacle. One year some of the young men purchased a five gallon can of coal oil and soaked the debris. The flames shot high into the heavens. Gathered around these camp fires old and young enjoy a season of merriment. Usually a program of readings is prepared interspersed with songs.

For a number of years past the Union Christian Endeavor Association has held their summer conference in the Turner tabernacle. During the last week of August these grounds are an ideal place for such a retreat. These meetings have been well patronized and they constitute a physical, mental and moral refreshment for all young people who will attend.

At the convention in 1928 resolutions were passed asking the program committee for the following year to make place for a Christian Endeavor Conference for our own young people during the sessions of the convention. The result of this appeal remains for some future historian to record.

The real strength of the State Endeavor work was when the societies were centering their attention on the up-building of our own societies. In late years there has been a tendency for Endeavorers to give the Union work the preference. While this has had some wholesome reactions, yet it has been largely at the expense of our own work. Practically no money is being raised now for Christian Endeavor representing Churches of Christ. The union movement is liberally patronized by our own societies. This is not meant as a criticism on union Endeavor work, for the author is heartily in favor of it. But he dares to depart from the rôle of historian long enough to prophesy that when Christian Endeavorers of Churches of Christ shall adopt an aggressive policy of work that will involve the special mission and message of Disciples of Christ they will again come into prominence for the attendance at state conventions and the enthusiasm that characterized former gatherings of young people.

CHAPTER XIII

IN LANDS BEYOND

The people known as Disciples of Christ have risen to missionary heights through travail of soul. In the early days of the movement a world vision was but vaguely experienced. Perhaps the persecution encountered centered effort on self-establishment in the homeland. Whatever may have been the cause, or causes, of an o-missionary atmosphere it will always be a matter of regret that the movement was 40 years old before missionary sentiment was crystallized into organized effort. Likewise, it should be a matter for profound gratefulness that when it did become crystallized it was sponsored and led by that matchless Christian character, Alexander Campbell. From the time of its organization in 1849 until the time of his death Alexander Campbell was the honored president of the American Christian Missionary Society.

At the time of beginning of organized missions by Disciples of Christ in 1849 there were only five organized congregations of Christians only in Oregon. The first congregation had been planted only three years before. So the history of our cause in Oregon is almost synonymous with the history of organized missions among us as a people.

With this background it is not strange that Oregon did not become tremendously enthusiastic over missions in her beginning days. Was it not itself a mission field? Did not these pioneers have enough to do to establish the cause at home? Besides, the incomes of these hardy pioneers was of such a character that contributions of any kind were a difficult matter except such as could be paid in "keep." Salaries were not paid to ministers in those days, so why should they be expected to send money to convert the heathen? The high point of the gospel, in those days, was found in Acts 2:38. Matthew 28:18-20 had not yet soaked into the consciousness of the churches except as it referred to Jerusalem and Judea. And 1 Corinthians 16: 1, 2 had not yet been heard about.

We must judge people by the light they have, so we will not be critical of those noble men and women of God in the infancy of Oregon discipledom for not seeing as clearly as we of this latter day. But gradually the missionary motive grew. Here and there a soul was brave enough to declare in bugle tones that even Oregon should have a share in world evangelization. Occasionally a preacher had the temerity to "pass the hat." It always brought back something. But Oregon disciples were about as long coming to a realization of their missionary obligation as were their fathers in the faith in the beginning.

In the *Christian Herald* of January 27, 1888, we find this comment from an unnamed contributor (perhaps the editor):

"There are 44 churches in Oregon. Last year these sent contributions for the support of the work carried on by the Foreign Society. They gave in all $22.35. The church at Amity gave $8.15, or more than one-third of the entire amount."

In the same issue, over the signature of J. W. Webb, then one of the leading preachers in the state, we find this statement:

"In the proceedings of the General Missionary Society I see there were only about three contributors from Oregon toward sending the gospel outside its own borders. Brethren, are we so poor that we can do so little towards fulfilling the Great Commission 'Preach the gospel to every creature?' "

These excerpts are presented with a twofold purpose: First, to show the lack of missionary conscience in those early days; and, Second, to show that there were those who were fully alive to this phase of the gospel. It is not spoken critically, but a historian must record the facts regardless of their favorable, or unfavorable, character. Then, too, they serve to emphasize the transformation that has taken place in latter years in a missionary way. It is with a considerable degree of pride that the following facts are presented. Perhaps pride in this instance may be pardoned, since it is an unselfish one.

I. LOCAL MISSIONS

From the beginning Oregon has had a considerable foreign population. From time to time the hearts of the people have been exercised over this matter and efforts have been made to do our duty by the "stranger within our gates." Nearly every race under heaven has found asylum in Oregon. In some sections rural communities have been bought up by foreigners. They have colonized in the cities. Astoria is populated by a large majority of foreign birth. Effort has been made to preach the gospel to these people, yet it must be admitted that the effort has not been commensurate with the task.

1. The first effort along this line was the Chinese Mission in Portland, mentioned in another chapter. This was started in 1891. At that time there was a large, and growing, Chinese population in Portland. That seemed to be the most favorable point of attack for the gospel in the homeland. Accordingly the First Church in Portland, in connection with the Christian Woman's Board of Missions, began work among them. Enthusiasm rose to

great heights at times. In its brightest day a mission building was planned and even considerable money was raised to that end. But the growing restrictions on Chinese immigration caused the Chinese population in Portland to decrease and it never seemed expedient to erect the building. The Mission continued until 1924. There are Chinese in Portland yet whose lives were brightened for all time to come, and who still remember with gratitude the blessed days spent in the Chinese Christian Mission room.

2. The records show that in 1892 a mission was started among the Swedes of Portland by A. Erickson. This was short lived. There are no documents concerning it except the bare record of it on the church roll of the State Board. We do not find anyone who can speak for it beyond the fact that the effort was made. It was an independent work, apart from the assistance of Mission Boards, yet it belonged to the Brotherhood. While it failed as we count success, it indicates that there was kept alive that missionary passion without which a church is not a Church of Christ.

3. In 1915 Bruce Wolverton, with the aid of the First Church in Portland, started a work among the Armenians of that city. Quite a number were drawn together, but for some reason it did not continue long. The First Church of Portland has the honor of having among its membership a number of earnest Armenian Christians, some of them successful and prosperous merchants of the city. In its membership, too, was G. N. Shishmanian, one of the first missionaries sent out by the Foreign Society to a foreign land—Turkey. He died in the membership of this congregation.

II. Beyond the Borders

1. Nellie Clark, of Salem, was the first representative from Oregon to foreign lands. She went to China in 1904. She was compelled to return because of ill health.

2. J. J. Handsaker and his wife went to Jamaica in 1905. They continued there about a year and a half then returned to the states. Brother Handsaker has, since his return, accomplished phenomenal work for the Near East Relief.

3. Everard Moon and his wife were the next to go out. Originally they came from the church at Kelso, Washington. He received his preparation and inspiration for missionary service in Eugene Bible University, and did some Sunday School and evangelistic work before going to Africa in 1908. With the exception of furlough periods they have been in continuous service.

4. W. L. Mellinger and his wife went to Mexico in 1909 to take charge of educational work at Monterrey. They left the Woodlawn (Portland) church to respond to this call. They spent four years there and returned only because the civil war made it necessary for Americans to leave the country.

5. J. Carlos Ghormley was the son of our veteran preacher J. F. Ghormley. Carl had fully determined not to walk in his father's footsteps, but to be a doctor instead. After commencing his preparation for a medical career he met W. G. Menzies, who was home from India on furlough, and his soul was fired with a desire to go back with him. Accordingly he, with his wife and family, left in 1909 for India, where they spent nearly five years. They came home to complete the medical course,

and left a little girl buried in Indian soil. After finishing
school the war came on, Carl enlisted, and fate decreed
that he should not get back to the mission field.

6. Effie McCallum went from the First Church in Eugene to China in 1915. It was in the atmosphere of a
Christian home (her father was pastor of the Eugene
Church for 13 years) and the Eugene Bible University
that she received the missionary passion. She remained
on the mission field for more than one term of service then
married a fellow-missionary, W. R. Bacon, and returned
to the States where they are engaged in Christian service.

7. Goldie Wells went to Africa in 1920. She is an all
Oregon girl, and a splendid example of what a girl can
do toward accomplishing the biggest task in the world.
She caught the missionary vision in the little church at
Halsey, and through many difficulties worked her way
through school in preparation for this service. She is
still in the harness on the Congo.

8. David Byerlee and his wife are both Oregon young
people—he from the St. Johns (Portland) Church, and
she from Salem First. They went to Africa in 1920.
Brother Byerlee left a lucrative job as a printer to ac-
cept a poorly paid job as a missionary. He uses his
printer's craft in missionary work and the poor salary
is not counted a sacrifice. During his first furlough home
David said to the author: "Brother Swander, you do
not know it but I was once opposed to missionary work.
I heard you give a missionary sermon one day and it
changed my whole attitude toward missions." How great
an oak comes from so little an acorn! The writer was

pleading that day for a missionary offering, and Lo! it was greater than he knew until twelve years later.

9. The year 1920 also took another of Oregon's consecrated girls, Edna Whipple, who went that year to China. While there she married a fellow-missionary, Mr. Gish, who was tragically drowned. Mrs. Gish was transferred to the Philippines when the war in China drove out the missionaries.

10. James H. McCallum was a brother to Effie. He went to China in 1921 and remained until the missionaries were compelled to evacuate their posts by reason of civil war. It was his heart's desire to return to China, or go elsewhere in the service of Christ, but the funds of the Society were in embarrassing condition and Jamie graciously offered to relieve them by locating with a church in the states.

11. Kenneth Hendricks and his wife sailed for Japan in 1921. His early years were spent in the little church at Gladstone, while his wife was an Idaho girl. He prepared for the ministry in Eugene Bible University, and volunteered for missionary service at a state convention. He comes from forbears that make great missionaries. They are both still on the field.

12. Elmer Boyer went to Africa in 1921. He was the product of the little Bethel Church in Polk county, one of the pioneer churches in the state. The church's life went out some years ago, but its light shines on. Though dead in Oregon, it continues to live and preach the message in Africa. His wife also was an Oregon product.

13. Hattie Mitchell was a little girl with hair ribbons in the Ashland church when the author first knew her.

Just where and when the missionary passion seized her it is hard to say, but one knowing the family suspects it was at her mother's knee. Anyway it was planted, it was watered, and God is giving it increase in darkest Africa. She went to the foreign field in 1922.

14. Grace N. Young honored her Lord by going to Tibet in 1923. She was educated, heart and mind, in Eugene Bible University. When God called she replied, "Here am I, Lord, send me."

Those mentioned above all went out under the auspices of a Missionary Board. There are those who have listened to the call of missions apart from our General Societies. They, too, have been the flower of our youth and we do them honor by recording their names alongside the rest.

15. Ralph Isaacson and his wife "Bunny" are properly California products, but we claim them because they were Oregon educated. They served in the Cunningham Mission, Japan, until 1928, when they came home on furlough. They will not return.

16. Cecile Harding also joined the forces in Japan in the Cunningham Mission.

17. Rose Bothwell went to China but came home when the civil war compelled missionaries to leave.

18. Maude Whipple also went to China but her work was interrupted by war.

19. Lewis C. Martin looked upon stricken Europe as a mission field after his graduation from Eugene Bible University. Unable to secure employment there with his own people he accepted a commission from the Congregational Board as a teacher in Bulgaria.

20. Zenas Olson is the product of another abandoned

country church—Farmington. His parents live at Hillsboro. He accepted service under a denominational board.

Apart from these there are others who deserve honorable mention in this missionary roster. Mrs. Maude Madden, the veteran missionary to Japan, is counted an Oregonian. She has taken school work at Eugene and they count this as their American headquarters. Dr. Victor Rambo, in India, belongs to Oregon in affection at least. His parents, Mr. and Mrs. W. E. Rambo, of Portland, were missionaries in India when Victor was born. They have labored in Oregon for a dozen years. Because of this, Oregon desires to claim part ownership to him.

This is a worthy list. Every one is a credit to the state, and they are evidence that Oregon believes, and obeys, the Great Commission. The list is destined to grow larger. Our fear is that in searching out names that belong on the roll we may inadvertantly have missed some one. If such should be the case the author begs that he be notified of it that future lists may be corrected. The story of missions is vastly different now from what it was in 1849.

III. Story of "The Oregon"

We have often been asked for a written story of the "Oregon." It has never before been put in complete form, but a history of what Oregon has done for regions beyond would not be complete without it. We are presuming to give it here in exact detail.

At the state convention in 1908, at Turner, Dr. Royal J. Dye and his wife, from Africa, were present. On the last Sunday morning Dr. Dye addressed a vast audience on his favorite theme—Africa. In vivid language he pictured some of the hardships of the missionary, and particularly he dwelt upon the difficulties of travel from one place to another. There were no roads through the jungles except trails, and these were beset with swamps and wild beasts. The only open highway through the whole country was the great Congo River. Handmade canoes, manned by native rowers, were the only means of navigation. The river was infested with alligators, and the current was swift. If they escaped one danger they would run into another, so that in a very real sense they were always between Scylla and Charybdis. He said that a steamboat, sufficient for the use of the mission, would solve many problems both in the matter of safety and efficiency. One could be built for $15,000 but the Society did not have the money.

The address made a profound impression. During the noon hour folks were telling each other how sorry they were for the poor missionary and how they wished they had that boat. It remained for a young student for the ministry, James Blood, to say how much he was sorry. Though only a student he had a note for $150 due him and he would gladly give that toward the building of a boat. James Blood never became a preacher from the platform, but that simple word of his that day has preached the gospel to more heathen, and brought more souls to a knowledge of Christ, than he could have done had he spent his life time as a preacher.

Brother Blood's statement was repeated to the author by Harry Trumbull Sutton, acting head of the School of Oratory at Eugene Bible University. After discussing the possibility of raising $15,000 for such a purpose we went to Dr. Dye and talked it over with him. We then

called upon Davis Errett, president of the State Board
that year, and in counsel with him decided that the matter should be laid before the audience that afternoon. It
was stipulated with Dr. Dye that the boat should be
named the "Oregon" if the Oregon churches decided to
undertake the task of raising the money. That afternoon
Mrs. Dye gave an uplifting address, at the close of which
32 young people volunteered for Christian service. The
congregation then partook of the Lord's Supper with
quickened hearts and moist eyes. After that service Davis
Errett spoke with persuasive voice concerning the need
that Dr. Dye had voiced at the morning hour, he told of
the offer made by Brother Blood, and the decision of a few
to put it before the convention. The responsive "Aye!"
was unanimous. In a few minutes $2,132 was pledged as
an earnest of the action. George C. Ritchey, pastor of
the church at Newberg, was appointed by the convention
to present the matter to the churches and ask for funds
with which to build the boat.

Through the coming year Brother Ritchey pressed the
matter with vigor. The churches took hold eagerly. It
was a big task for Oregon in those days to raise $15,000
for any purpose. About $10,000 was actually raised in
Oregon. The effort was a challenge to others. Offers
of assistance came in from other states and the full amount
was pledged. The Foreign Society accepted Oregon's offer at face value and let the contract for construction
of the boat which was made ready for dedication at the
Centennial Convention in Pittsburgh, in 1909. The dedication of the "Oregon" was one of the chief events at
that convention.

The boat was shipped to Africa "knocked down." E. R. Moon, Oregon's missionary was there to receive Oregon's boat. He had the task of putting it together and for a long time he was "Captain" Moon.

The real worth of the "Oregon" will never be fully recorded. It has not only taken the missionaries safely over the waters of Africa's great river, but it has enabled them to do vastly more work than could be humanly possible without it. It has saved freight charges and has even earned freight rates. It has hastened the doctor to distant points and saved life. It has increased the respect of the native for the white man. Its full worth will never be recorded.

The fruitage of a deed is scarcely ever measured by the direct product of that act. The greatest fruitage of the "Oregon" is perhaps nothing that the "Oregon" itself has directly accomplished. But the story of the "Oregon," and its use on that river, reacted upon the hearts of loving men and women in two different states, so that today, instead of one boat on the Congo, she has two companions sailing on missions of mercy—the "Illinois" and the "Missouri." These companion boats are much larger and more efficiently equipped than the "Oregon," but every Oregonian is proud of the fact that our state paved the way.

For nearly twenty years the "Oregon" did service uninterruptedly. Then our hearts were saddened by the news that the government had demanded certain repairs and improvements to be made if it was to be continued in service. This would cost about $3,000. Again Oregon disciples accepted the challenge and Dr. Dye was sent to the state to present the cause before the churches and receive gratuities therefor. It was a glad day when word came from Dr. Dye that Oregon had gone over the top. This was done in 1927.

Out of 44 churches in 1889 only three contributed to world missions: out of the 127 churches in 1927 there were probably not more than a dozen that did not have some fellowship in the work of world missions. There are fervent souls who pray that the time will come when history will record a unanimous state in support of a world-wide program.

CHAPTER XIV

CHRISTIAN STEWARDSHIP

The phrase "Christian Stewardship," as referring to the Christian's financial responsibility to the kingdom of God, is a modern conception. It is an illustration of the fact that truth is not all perceived at a glance, but that in the life of each man, and in the life of each generation, there comes a conviction of things not before seen.

Had this phrase been used in referring to money in the early days of Oregon history the speaker would doubtless have been regarded as an innovator of a dangerous type. These pioneer disciples in Oregon were not "antis" by any manner of means; yet, in their minds, money was a carnal thing and was not to be linked up with the preaching of sermons, baptizing people, and observing the Lord's Supper. Money was scarce, consequently collections would necessarily be scanty even if the spirit were willing. Salvation was without money and without price—literally, nakedly so. Ministers did not receive salaries, but worked for a living with their own hands. It may be subject for debate whether they worked for a living because they received no support for preaching, or whether they received no salaries because they did work for a living. Perhaps it was both. But one fact remains very plain—the church did not receive instruction concerning financial obligations to the kingdom.

This failure was pardonable in the beginning, but as time went on it increasingly left its impress upon the work as people became more prosperous and able to bestow

goods upon the kingdom. One of the best statements of
the financial situation of that early day comes from the
pen of J. V. Crawford, a pioneer of 1851, a preacher
who knew from experience whereof he spoke, and who
will always live in the memory of the author as one of
God's chosen men. He says:

"The minister preached for no stipulated salary, and the voluntary contributions were very small, as no public collections were
taken. Preachers supported themselves and their families by other
labor, usually on the farm, while they preached the gospel 'free
gratis for nothing.' To that custom we are indebted, in no small
degree, for the niggardly parsimony now rife in many of our
churches. They were true to the Book, however, and hewed to
the line, letting the chips fall where they would. They never failed
to declare the whole counsel of God as they understood it. . . . .
and woe to the witless 'sectarian' wight who unsheathed his sword
in an attack on their position."

It is correctly surmised that the writer of this excerpt
was not affected by the "parsimony" mentioned in the
letter. Brother Crawford was an extremely broadminded
man, charitable to champion and antagonist alike, and supported the church "as much as in him" was in an un-
usually liberal manner. But not all those early pioneers
escaped the effects of the failure to preach the gospel according to gold. One good pioneer brother, whose heart
and life were pure gold, would squirm like an eel under
a sermon that dealt with the pocketbook. One time a
representative of the American Society came to his church
to represent Home Missions, and was entertained in his
home. He was extraordinarily interested in the plea for
"home" missions, and promised to give liberally when the
offering was taken. The visitor was delighted and mentioned it to the pastor of the church in extravagant terms.
He had hope of receiving several hundred dollars. The
pastor, knowing his parishioner better than the visiting

brother, said, "Yes, I wouldn't be surprised if he gave twice as much for Home Missions as he did for Foreign Missions."

"And how much was that?" asked the visitor.

"Two bits," replied the pastor.

The visitor was indignant; he was insulted; the good brother was insulted. The pastor was justly rebuked for his lack of faith. The pastor made no reply but went on preparing for the Home Missionary offering. He preached passionately for the evangelizing of America. He distributed the envelopes with care and pleaded earnestly for every member to put in a generous offering. He made every preparation in common use in those days. When the envelopes were finally gathered in he curiously sought out the old gentleman's envelope to see what his offering actually was. Sure enough! There it was, as plain as anything—a four-bit piece of silver sealed tightly within!

This same good brother had sojourned with his family in another community for several years. He refused to take his church membership with him. One day two members of these two churches happened to meet and were comparing notes about their mutual friend and brother, and it came out that while the good brother lived in the land of the sojourning he refused to contribute to the church on the ground that his membership was at the other place and he had to contribute there. They arranged between them that he should receive a solicitation from the other place and see what his reply to that would be. When it came he replied that he lived at the other place and had to support there. This comparison of notes revealed the further fact that while the good brother had sojourned away from home for ten years he had actually contributed

$10 to the kingdom of God. This good old man will have a place in the kingdom eternal, of this we feel assured, but it will not be because he was a "good steward" of God's wealth. He was simply unable to shake off the effect of early training, and later teaching and revelation of obligation failed to reach his heart. Had the early pioneers understood the eighth and ninth chapters of II Corinthians as well as they did Acts 2:38 the church would have a larger history to write today.

We do not wish to impute blame to the pioneers for a failure to instruct the church in kingdom finances. An apology has been left by one of their own number, R. G. Callison, who dropped dead while delivering an address at one of our state conventions. In it he says:

"There seems to be an idea in the minds of some of our present day preachers that the pioneers in their work failed in giving the proper instruction in the grace of giving in the early organization of the churches on this coast. They seem to forget that it took six months to make the trip across the plains from the Mississippi Valley with ox teams, hauling their supplies for the entire trip, and that at that time land was cheap, $1.25 per acre for raw land, and that it took all the immigrants could raise to outfit them for the trip, so that when they arrived on this western coast they were to bed rock.

"It is true that the government gave a donation of 320 acres to the man, and the same to his wife, until the early '50s, when the man received 160 acres and his wife the same; but a home and farm must be made, and so far as contribution for the ministry was concerned, it was almost out of the question.

"Therefore our ministers preached the gospel to the people without money and without price, in the schoolhouses, barns, private homes, and groves; the people gladly hearing the messages that were brought to them. In this way the scattered sheep were gathered together and churches organized."

Whatever may be the criticism justly passed upon that generation for its shyness at financial teaching, it at least would be well for the present generation to emulate that pioneer zeal that characterized our forbears in the gospel.

Gradually, however, the obligations of stewardship began to be acknowledged. As missionary information filtrated through the consciousness men's hearts were touched and generous gifts began to be made for kingdom purposes. Here and there a loving heart made it possible for a congregation to be fittingly housed. Generous gifts were occasionally made for missions. Perhaps the first gift on a large scale made in Oregon came from "Father" and "Mother" Turner, who provided the land for a home for camp meeting purposes, and upon which was later erected the tabernacle that has not been excelled in the whole state as a gathering place for the saints. This property had a valuation of perhaps $10,000 in that day, the equal of three times that amount in this day. Mrs. Cornelia Davis, a daughter of the Turners, has given a museum to Eugene Bible University worth several thousand dollars, and has erected a modern house of worship for the church at Turner at a cost of more than $40,000. In 1909 there came to the State Board the sum of $436.50 from the Henderson estate in Albany. A considerable sum was also left to the college at Eugene from the same estate. George Gerking, of Athena, paid the sum of $1,500 to state mission work during a period of five years, besides making heavy contributions to other causes. For several years a certain good woman, whose name we are under obligation to withhold, gave the entire missionary support for the state evangelist, G. E. Williams. In more recent times James A. Pointer, then a young man preparing for the ministry, gave the State Board $1,500, with which the work at Astoria was opened. Later Brother Pointer gave another contribution of nearly $1,000 to the Permanent Fund. Fannie Keyt, of Perrydale church, left by will $10,000 to the Woman's Missionary work. Mention cannot be made of the many gifts totalling into the hundreds of thousands of dollars through annuities into the work of the Eugene Bible University. God knows them and will honor them with a bejeweled crown of life. These things are tokens of a quickening conscience on stewardship.

Aggressive teaching on stewardship among Disciples of Christ in Oregon is a comparatively recent thing. From time to time isolated instances of it could be found, but no concerted effort was made to indoctrinate the church with its responsibility before God concerning money until 1917. The author of these pages was asked to prepare a paper for the Northwest Pacific Preachers' Parliament, to be held in Eugene in December of that year, on the subject of tithing. He named the paper "God's Share."

The writer had been a tither for many years. As a background to his own convictions, and as a prelude to the story of this propaganda, it seems not out of order here to present a brief sketch of the author's experience in becoming a tither and how he came to the position outlined in the paper. He gives it here exactly as he wrote it for another purpose, and that will explain the use of the first person pronoun.

How I Became a Tither

1. I was the Superintendent of a Sunday school. It was Children's Day for Foreign Missions, and I was debating with myself long and seriously whether I should give two-bits or four-bits. Finally, the four-bit piece won, thank God, but I was not satisfied with myself.

2. Soon afterwards a tract on tithing fell into my hands. It was written by an Adventist, and of course it was unorthodox. How could tithing be Scriptural for a Christian! And how dared one

to tithe if it was unscriptural! But gradually it became apparent to me that it was not necessarily *anti-scriptural*, even though it might be unscriptural. No! Then why not try it for a time and see if it gave more satisfaction than pinching a quarter or a half dollar until the eagle squawked! I yielded to the suggestion simply as an expedient.

3. Result: I never had any more scandals in my soul on Missionary day. Then, too, I could always figure ahead about how much I could give to any Christian cause. The joy of giving increased and occasionally I grew extravagant and gave beyond the tenth.

4. While beginning to tithe simply as an experiment, and continuing it as an expedient, I began preaching it to others. But I was continually met with the objection that it was unscriptural— an objection I never could answer. This led me to a more careful examination of the Scriptures on this subject with the following result:

(1) I found that the Scriptures declare that "the earth is the Lord's and the fulness thereof"; that God never gave man *ownership* of the earth, but simply "dominion" over it. That makes God the *owner*, and man only God's trustee of worldly wealth. It was quite a jolt to learn that I couldn't actually *own* the earth; but it was some consolation to know that nobody else could either.

(2) Somehow it then filtered into my consciousness that man has always recognized the owner's right to a share of the increase made on his property, and that the owner himself has a right to name what that share shall be. That being true God had a RIGHT to a share of earth's increase since He was the sole owner thereof; and He also had the right to say how much that share should be.

(3) Searching to find out if God had ever declared what His share should be I discovered that as far back as the history of civilized man (or uncivilized, either) tithes had been paid to the god of that people. Tithes were a custom before the birth of the Hebrew nation. God had said to the Jews, "The tithe is holy unto Jehovah." No other share is ever mentioned in God's Word as being holy to Him, or as belonging to Him. It was another jolt to discover that I hadn't been as loyal to my God as the heathen had been to his.

(4) But the Law of Moses was abolished, and was not the tithe abolished with it? So folks argued, and I had to give a grudging Amen! Then another fact dawned upon me—that the tithe did not exist by virtue of the Law. It belonged to Jehovah by divine right, not by fiat of law. The Law recognized this and simply declared the divine ownership of the tithe just the same as it declared the divine ownership of the heavens and the earth. It had always been His, and always would be, for it was "holy" unto

Him. When the Law was abolished the tithe was no more abolished than was God's ownership of the earth which was also declared by the same Law. It became clear, too, that tithing was one of the marks of the priesthood of Melchizedek which Christ came to restore. Therefore, Christ had the same right to the tithe as did Melchizedek.

(5) A further study revealed the fact that the early churches practiced tithing for nearly three hundred years before they were swallowed up with the greed that came with the apostacy. I began to feel happy and secure at last in the Scripturalness of tithing.

5. As I came more and more in contact with people who tithed I noted the satisfaction they had in it. I saw that tithers always gave more in proportion to their means than other folks. I remembered that I had never heard a word of dissatisfaction with tithing from one who tithed; the criticsm always came from those who did not. Some, I found who had once tithed and quit it; but from them, even, there was no complaint—the complaints always came from those who wouldn't try it.

6. Then I began to figure on what tithing would do. The United States Census Bureau said that the average income of every man, woman and child in the United States was $500 per annum. To be safe I figured it at $300. Upon that basis the income of a church of 100 members would be $30,000; the tithe of that income would be $3,000. The income of the 20,000 disciples in Oregon would be approximately $6,000,000; the tithe of that would be $600,000. Yet the latest figures on Oregon's benevolences is not more than one-third of that. Tithing would more than double the salary of every minister and missionary, pay off our debts in short time, and permit us to have the necessary equipment for our work, besides expanding our work many fold. It would surely pay.

In the paper read before the Parliament these facts were elaborated at considerable length. The Parliament received it with favor and a resolution was presented, and unanimously adopted, asking for its publication in tract form. One preacher, more practical than others, suggested that it would cost money to print a tract, and that it would be no more than fair that those voting for the publication should then and there make a definite subscription for them to give it solid backing. As an evidence of good faith more than 3,000 were subscribed for that day. An edition of 5,000 was published, which was quickly exhausted. It was revised in some respects and a second edition was published, which was also quickly exhausted. A third edition was printed and that has been generously called for, only a few yet remaining at this writing.

In the fall of 1921 the United Christian Missionary Society sent into the state a team of workers consisting of W. F. Turner, E. S. Muckley, and Mrs. Louise Kelly, who toured the churches in company with the state secretary in the interest of missionary education and Christian Stewardship. Many tithers were enrolled.

The following year Roy K. Roadruck, C. E. Benlehr, A. O. Kuhn, and Mrs. Eda T. Moore were sent upon a similar mission. Many tithers were again enrolled.

At the 1922 state convention George F. Bradford, from California, was present with a series of stewardship addresses. He also visited a few of the churches before returning. This visit resulted in signing up a limited number of tithers.

At a later period the State Secretary delivered a series of stewardship studies at the Leadership Training School, which was a part of the state convention program, and which he afterwards delivered in many of the churches. The Pentecostal campaign program has as one of its aims the enrollment of 5,000 tithers by Pentecost 1930.

CHAPTER XV

THE PERMANENT FUND

"We need a Permanent Fund," declared Morton L. Rose in the President's address at the convention of 1899. It was a little seed cast out into a great unfallowed field. It did not immediately take root and grow—nor did birds pick it up, nor did thorns and thistles choke it. A seed germ does not readily lose its vitality. Nor did this little seed. It was a long time in germinating, so long in fact that the hearer of that pronouncement would long afterward have declared that it was sterile.

There is no further record of the mention of a Permanent Fund for many years. Doubtless, though, it was in the minds of many brethren from time to time. But the immediate need was greater than the immediate income, and it was doubtless felt that until present needs were more nearly satisfied it was useless to attempt to pile up a revenue for the future.

When the author of this volume became Secretary in 1908 he became convinced that the ultimate future of Oregon Missions would depend upon a stable income from a permanent source. He began to talk it among the brethren. It was ten years before the talk bore fruit. In June of 1918 the East Oregon Convention was held at The Dalles. G. E. Williams, pastor at Bend, came to the convention with a $50 Liberty Bond which the church at Bend was sending to the State Board. The Secretary seized upon this incident for the creation of a Permanent Fund. The suggestion met with favor both in the Bend church and in the State Board. When the gift was announced to the convention pledges of War Savings stamps and cash were made to the amount of $85.00 more. At the convention in Turner the next month the Future Work Committee report carried a resolution that a ''Permanent Fund be raised,'' which was unanimously adopted by the convention. Quite a considerable increase to the Fund was made in pledges and cash at this meeting, and the Permanent Fund was definitely launched.

The missionary year of 1918-19 was started with $50 to the credit of the Permanent Fund. During that following twelve months there was received from donations $286.03; from the Men and Millions Movement (a percentage of whose receipts from Oregon came back to the state), $196.41; transferred from an Emergency Fund, $92.87; and from interest earnings, $10.37. The total at the end of the first year was $635.68 in the Fund.

It is the place here to explain the ''Emergency Fund,'' from whence came one item of the receipts. During the years previous to 1917 it was the usual thing to have an empty treasury at some time during the year, which necessitated borrowing from the bank until sufficient money came in from the offerings to repay it. The State Board conceived the idea of establishing a reserve fund that would be sufficient to tide over such emergencies. Thus it was called an ''Emergency Fund.'' Its money was to be borrowed only, and repaid when the offerings justified. Interest was to be paid on it just the same as on money borrowed from the bank. When not in use it was to be kept in a savings account at the customary interest. It was in reality a Permanent Fund, but could be used for one purpose only—loaning to the General Fund in case of emergency. Because of that limited use it was expected to lift the amount only to a few hundred dollars. When the real Permanent Fund was started the Board decided that the Emergency Fund was no longer necessary and voted to transfer its money to the Permanent Fund.

During the year 1919-20 increase was made to the Fund as follows: From new offerings, $31.50; interest earnings, $52.40; from James A. Pointer through the Men and Millions Movement, $992.04.

In the beginning of the year 1920-21 the State Board voted to turn all life membership gifts into the Permanent Fund. This was made retroactive for the previous year, and that turned $277.22 from that source into the Fund. In addition to that the receipts for the year were as follows: From life members, $155.00; other offerings, $35.00; memorial gifts, $25.00; interest earnings, $118.41; promissory notes, $100.00.

During the next year, 1921-22, the following addition to the Permanent Fund is noted: Life memberships, $94.00; Disciples' World Movement, $3.80; Men and Millions Movement, $3.16; interest earnings, $187.87; mortgage, $400.00. The mortgage was one given by the Montavilla (Portland) church for money they had borrowed from the Joint Board of Christian Churches of Portland in 1915, and upon which no interest had ever been paid. This default in interest was not the fault of the church. They had had a struggle financially, it was agreed that the mortgage should be the last of their obligations to be paid, a claim for interest had never been presented, and in the meantime the personnel of the Church Board had changed to an extent that many of them did not even know of the obligation while the few old members who remained had forgotten about it. As the time drew near when the note would be outlawed the Secretary called the attention of the State Board to it. The Board voted to transfer the mortgage to the Permanent Fund and authorized the Secretary to make such an adjustment on the interest as would be within the ability of the church to pay and thus save the note from outlawry. The matter was presented to the Church Board, and they graciously acknowledged the obligation. About $140 interest was due. An offer was made to give a receipt for interest in full upon payment of $50. The church responded with alacrity and, in addition to paying this amount on interest, also paid $25 on the principal. They continued to pay from time to time until finally in December, 1926, the last payment was made and the mortgage was released.

During the next year, 1922-23, increase to the Fund was as follows: life memberships, $30.00; interest earnings, discounts and premiums, $246.74.

The next year, 1923-24, the following was added; life memberships, $15.00; other offerings, $5.00; interest earnings, $207.05.

The following year, 1924-25, we find the following: offerings, $10.00; interest earnings, $217.45.

In 1925-26 the records show as follows: offerings, $9.80; trust funds, $60.16; liberty bond, $50.00; interest earnings, $242.07. The trust fund indicated above was money that was on hand in the Seaside church treasury when they disbanded. They wished to dispose of it so a future church there might benefit by it. Our Board assured them that they could place it in our Permanent Fund and if a church were ever started there again the Board would return the money to it.

The year 1926-27 gave increase to the Fund only of interest earnings in the amount of $258.11.

The year 1927-28 to date of writing (June 30, 1928) yields the following new money: Interest, $222.97; offerings, $5.00; sale of property, $75.00. The sale of property indicated above was the Riverview church lot on the highway between Junction City and Eugene. This is mentioned in another chapter. The church disbanded before erecting a house on the lot. The real estate was deeded to the State Board. It became evident that there would probably never be a church house built on this property, a chance came to dispose of it, which was done and the money placed in the Permanent Fund with the reservation that in case a Church of Christ ever was built in that neighborhood the money might be returned to it.

There never has been any special effort made for increasing the Permanent Fund. Two leaflets have been printed and distributed, "The Permanent Fund," and "Reasons for a Permanent Fund." Attention has been called to it from time to time in the monthly *Bulletin*. Those especially interested in it are hoping for a propitious time when a real campaign can be waged for the Fund looking to the increasing of it to $100,000.

The reasons for a Permanent Fund may be stated as follows: The stability of any institution is dependent upon the stability of its foundation. Missionary offerings are fluctuating in character. Some years there are flood tides in receipts, and other years there are ebb tides without any apparent reason therefor. The Board never knows exactly what its income may be until the end of the year. Its expense budget must be accepted at the beginning of the year. During the months of July, August, September and October there is very little in the way of offerings coming into the treasury. With a sufficient Permanent Fund that would be giving a regular amount of interest the Board would be much better able to take up the shrinkage in years of ''ebb tide,'' while the years of ''flood tide'' would permit an expansion through the interest earnings. It would enable the Board to measure its ability for the year ahead with much more certainty of what it will have to spend. The local church begins its year by pledging up its membership for one year in advance. The State Board has to contract with its corps of missionaries without a dollar pledged. The Permanent Fund would permit the Board to make up a respectable budget with much more confidence, and upon a larger scale, than it could possibly do without.

The ultimate goal of the Permanent Fund is $100,000, the convention having so voted. The Fund has not been without its opposition, though not serious. At the convention in 1919 the matter came up for debate and the declaration was boldly made upon the floor that the State Board had no use for such a fund, that it was a dangerous thing to put such a fund in the hands of a State Board, and strongly recommended that the present funds amounting to near $2,000 should be turned into evangelistic channels and used up. The argument was easily met and, when the vote was taken, the voice for the Fund was overwhelming.

The State Board has pledged its honor to a safe and sound policy in handling the Fund. Only securities of gilt edge character will be purchased. Speculative properties will not be considered for a moment. Investments will not be made with a view to reaping large profits from increased values, but only such investments as offer a safe and definite return. The investment of the funds is left in the hands of a committee especially appointed for that task. Upon that committee sits a banker of known integrity and sympathy of heart. No security is purchased without his endorsement. It is not altogether improbable that at some time they may make an investment that may not prove sound or profitable. The most careful business man makes such errors at times. The policy of the Committee is to place investments in small amounts rather than to tie it all up in one thing. Then, if any particular investment proves unwise, it will affect only a small portion of the Fund. At the present time $1,000 is the largest amount in one investment. Sums of $500 are preferred as investment units.

The State Board will receive anything of value for the Fund—bonds, notes, mortgages, real estate, buildings, jewels, cash—anything that has value, or is the evidence of value. If anything is received that does not appear to possess a stable value it will be turned into cash as soon as possible at the best possible figure and reinvested in securities of stable character. Notes received for the Fund will not be sold unless expressly agreed to by the signer, as the Board will not embarrass anyone who tries to assist the Fund by giving a note. Real estate or chattels will not be held in that form longer than necessary to convert their value into other securities.

The Permanent Fund is a safe investment for missionary money. In it your missionary money will go on yielding a missionary income year after year, yet the original dollar is left intact to go on working for the Master as long as time shall last. Thus one may know that long after his bones have crumbled to dust his money, when placed in the Permanent Fund, will be helping to evangelize the world.

Gifts for the Permanent Fund should be made payable to the *Oregon Christian Missionary Convention*, and sent to its offices in Portland, Oregon.

On the first day of July, 1928, the records of the Permanent Fund showed the following assets as they were then invested:

Promissory notes _ _ _ _ _ _ _ _		$ 125.00
Bonds:	Grants Pass Irrigation District _	1,000.00
	City of Redmond _ _ _ _ _	500.00
	First Christian Church Portland _	100.00
	City of Forest Grove _ _ _ _	500.00
	Salmon River Highway District _	500.00
	City of Cottage Grove _ _ _ _	500.00
	Liberty Bond _ _ _ _ _ _	50.00
Stock: Portland Electric Power Co. _ _ _		200.00
Cash in Savings Bank 4% Interest _ _ _		1,397.72

$4,872.72

CHAPTER XVI

IN THE LIFE OF A SECRETARY

This chapter must necessarily be quite personal, so the reader is asked to indulge the author in the use of the first person pronoun throughout the narrative. This chapter is included in the hope that it may unite a bit closer the bond of sympathy between the people and their servant who is universally known as the State Secretary.

I can truly say that the honor of the state secretaryship was thrust upon me. It was not a position of my own choice or seeking. I was happily located with one of the best churches in the state, and in one of the choicest towns in the state. The work was growing satisfactorily. It was against the earnest protest of many in the congregation that I left them.

I came to the state of Oregon from Nebraska in November, 1904. I had come primarily to hold a meeting for my old boyhood friend, W. L. Mellinger, at Ashland. At the close of that meeting I received, unsolicited, an invitation to visit the church at McMinnville with a view to becoming its pastor. How they learned of me I never knew, for I was a stranger in a strange land, and was fully expecting to return to the Middle States where a number of open pulpits offered inducements. However, I was in no hurry to go back, so decided to respond to their invitation. It was on Christmas Sunday that I visited them. A week later I received an official invitation to become their pastor, and on the first Lord's Day in February, 1905, I began a pastorate that holds for me today some of the happiest memories of my life.

My first state convention in Oregon was that of 1905. F. E. Billington was elected that year to succeed J. J. Evans as State Secretary. Billington proved most popular in that capacity, and he could easily have continued in the position for life if he had so desired. During his second year he came to my study one day and expressed a desire to settle down and work out some Bible School theories in actual experience which were coming to him as a result of special study he was making of that theme. He said he had talked with a number of men over the state about his successor and there was a general agreement that I would make a satisfactory incumbent. He asked my consent to election that year, 1907. I gave the matter very serious consideration, but finally came to the conclusion that I loved my people and my work at McMinnville too dearly to separate myself from them. I refused to be considered and Billington was elected for a third year. During that third year he came to me again and said that he had definitely decided upon laying down the work in 1908 and begged me to consider it favorably. I told him to go out and find some one else who would be acceptable. I went ahead with my work and did not give the matter further consideration.

When the convention met in June, 1908, the Committee on Nominations came to me and told me that I was the only man they had under consideration for the place, and asked my permission to report my name as the nominee for Secretary. After interviewing a number of the brethren I finally told the Committee that if it were the wish of the convention that I should do the work of state secre-

tary I would yield my own personal desires in the matter.
This decision was made the harder because of the fact
that one of my own elders was a member of the Nominating Committee, and their action was taken against
his protest. I was accordingly elected. I fully expected
then to serve in this capacity for five years—no more, and
I hoped no less. Five years rolled by and there seemed
to be no good stopping place. The term has lengthened out
at this writing to twenty years.

In preparing myself for the ministry I had never
thought of serving in the capacity of a state secretary.
Had I had such expectation I think I could have prepared
myself along some different lines that would have been
of great advantage to me. My knowledge of state secretaries had been quite limited previously to becoming
one, but I had always been moved to a profound respect
for them. My relations with them had always been happy.
They were great and good men as I knew them, and I
never supposed it possible for me to attain such heights.
My first glimpse of a secretary was in Iowa. The first
convention of Disciples of Christ I ever attended was a
district convention at Clarinda, Iowa, in 1894. Abram
E. Cory, afterwards missionary to China, and later a secretary of the United Society, was the district secretary.
At that time Brother Cory was as tall as he is now and
only about one-fourth as thick (I speak only from memory. I never measured him). He was the busiest man in
the convention. I have never seen a more successful effort
at being in two places at once. I went back to my humble
little church with a report of the convention, and A. E.
Cory was the hero in my eyes.

A little later I went to Nebraska and entered college

at Cotner University. F. A. Bright was State Secretary
in addition to being the pastor of one of the largest
churches in the state. I met him at two conventions and
measured him as a big man. Succeeding him came W. A.
Baldwin who occupied the position of Nebraska's secretary for a dozen years or more. I became intimately acquainted with him through the association of his work
and mine. The more I knew of him the higher my estima-
tion of him arose. He was a real friend to the young
preacher. Coming to Oregon I first met the secretary at
my first convention. It was a case of love at first sight
(on my part). John J. Evans appealed to me at once.
I have never had cause to regret the attachment then
formed, nor has my estimate of the man lessened. Likewise F. E. Billington was a companionable, helpful friend
and brother, as true as steel, and faithful to the utter-
most. These associations with state secretaries had produced a most favorable impression on my mind as to the
quality and character it took to fill the office. It left
a deep concern in my mind as to my ability to measure
up to the ideal.

During my incumbency as State Secretary I have come
in personal contact with nearly all the incumbents of like
position in the United States. Uniformly they have been
a high type of manhood and capability. Some of them
have been criticised heavily, and in a few cases perhaps
justly so, for they were only fallible men; but, as a group,
the churches have made no mistake in the selection of men
to lead their missionary work in the state. My greatest
desire has been that I might measure up acceptably with
the rest of them. I have watched them come and go
throughout the years until at the present time (1928) I am

the oldest state secretary in point of service in the United
States.

For eleven of these twenty years I conducted the work
of the office in my own home, furnishing all the equipment
therefor except a Neostyle duplicator and a Blickensderfer
typewriter. (How anyone could use either of these for
eleven years without losing his religion is now a mystery
to me.) I have never had a stenographer to share my
load. Correspondence has been attended to personally
whether at home or on the road. It will be germane to
this chapter to mention some of the duties incident to a
Secretary's job.

The correspondence is no small part of the work. From
three to five thousand letters per year have been written.
I remember that when I went back home from the convention that elected me one of my deacons remonstrated with
me for taking up this work. "Anybody can write letters," he said. "Yes," I replied, "anybody can *write*
letters, but not everybody would know what to put in
them." I spoke that facetiously, but I have found it
truer than I knew then. There are times when one knows
scarcely what to say. Here is a letter asking counsel in
a time of difficulty; no blanket answer can be given, but
it must be answered in the light of circumstances. Here is
another that presents a heartrending plea for state help,
and it is difficult to write back and explain the Board's
inability so they will comprehend that it is literally true
and not just a subterfuge. Here is another that is asking
for a new preacher, and the state office is expected to
recommend one that is guaranteed to give satisfaction.
Here is a preacher who wants a church, and if he is not
satisfactorily fitted out the Secretary is withholding from

him his just due. Here is a church that wants to fire
a preacher and they send for the Secretary to pull their
chestnuts out of the fire. Here is another preacher who
sends for the Secretary to help him get his church organized and in working order. Here is one from a church
that cannot meet its financial obligations; they want the
Secretary to come and wave a magic wand and get the
money by some mysterious process. But here is another
that speaks a word of appreciation that brings a flush of
joy to his cheeks. It is like an oasis in a desert. They
all have to be answered, and the answers must be as
various as the letters. One thing I have tried to do with
all this correspondence—to be prompt in caring for it,
and to answer every letter that required one. One of the
appreciative words I have heard concerning my work as
secretary, and which I prize very highly, is this: ''When
I write to Swander I expect an answer back on the next
mail, and I get it.'' In a few cases I have failed to merit
this commendation, but in the main I have tried to hold
up to this standard.

A State Secretary has to do the bookkeeping for the
state work (in Oregon). This consists in keeping an accurate account of the receipts and expenditures, receipting
for all remittances, banking the funds, keeping the different funds separate from each other, writing the monthly
checks, preparing a statement for the auditor each month,
and procuring and filing a monthly report from the missionaries. When money is received it is entered first upon
a pocket cash book. This is the secretary's constant pocket
companion and with it he can tell you every remittance
he has received back to the first of the missionary year.
At the close of the month this is copied into the office

record. It is then posted upon the ledger and distributed to the appropriate accounts. The money is deposited in three different accounts—the General Fund, which is banked at present in the First National Bank of Portland; the Tabernacle Fund, which contains all money pertaining to the annual gathering at Turner, and is kept in the Turner State Bank at Turner; and the Permanent Fund, which contains all uninvested cash belonging to that fund, and is on deposit at 4 per cent compound interest in the Portland Trust and Savings Bank. An exact copy of these ledger accounts is furnished to the Treasurer each month who checks them over for accuracy in figures and compares each item of expense with the appropriate check that drew it out. All checks are signed both by the Secretary and the Treasurer.

During the first ten years of the present Secretaryship the printing for the state work was done in the commercial shops. After the purchase of the Multigraph in 1919 all the printing (except wall posters) was done in our own office until 1926, and that work fell to my lot. This was no inconsiderable item. It involved annually about 6,000 letterheads, 5,000 envelope returns, 5,000 convention programs, 1,000 16 page annual bulletins, 150 monthly bulletins, circular letters innumerable, tracts, leaflets, pledge cards, report blanks, and other items. With the growth of the work it became imperative that some of this should be shifted back to the commercial shops. In 1926 the bulletins and programs were taken back there. Other matter is still being printed in the office on the multigraph. Literally many hundreds of dollars have been saved to the expense fund in this way.

This is just a glimpse of the office duties proper. In

addition to this the State Secretary is expected to serve
on all kinds of committees, attend all kinds of meetings,
and give assistance to all kinds of movements. In the
beginning days I honestly tried to respond to all of these
calls. But it came to pass that these outside demands
were such a drain upon time and energy that I was compelled to refuse all except such as were most urgent and
important. I have realized the value of meeting and mingling with other people, or of joining hand and heart in
other movements, but a State Secretary who has no office
help must either decline some of these opportunities or
neglect the work he was chosen to perform. This office is
expected to keep a preachers' list corrected up-to-date,
and he is constantly called upon by such organizations as
the Anti-Saloon League, Near East Relief, W. C. T. U.,
etc., for a corrected list. Those are all worthy organizations and I have tried to give them such help with cheer-
fulness. In addition to that the state office is the only
avenue of communication with the United Society over
matters of general and mutual import. The State Society
does not have any organic connection whatever with the
United Society, or any other society, but it does maintain
a friendly cooperative spirit with any agency that is seeking to promote the kingdom of God. Hence, we are called
upon for much of the data from Oregon for the annual
Year Book. The statistical tables and the preachers' list
are sometimes difficult jobs. Here is a church that fails
to report; the Secretary is jealous for his state's record
so he writes again and again for the report. Maybe he
gets it finally and maybe he doesn't. Here is a preacher
whose name accidentally slips out of the list in transcrib-
ing and proof reading fails to catch the error. Woe betide

the Secretary who makes a mistake with a preacher's name!

Then there is the work of the Secretary in the field. First of all, constitutionally, he is expected to raise the money for state missions. In the beginning days the method commonly in vogue was that of setting a day when the Secretary could visit the church, present the cause of Oregon missions, and take an offering. Sometimes his Sundays for this task would be dated ahead several months in advance. It soon became apparent to me that this would never put Oregon missions on a sound financial basis. So I began to agitate the matter of the every member canvass for both local work and missions. I then began to assist in such canvasses in preference to taking the offering for state missions. The next step in the development of the finances was the teaching of stewardship, and the holding of stewardship rallies. In this type of work I have seen the offerings grow greater in proportion than the increase in membership of the churches, so I count the effort a success. At the present time I do not take many offerings, yet there are still some churches on that basis, nor do I conduct so many canvasses as formerly; but my field time is rather devoted to building up missionary sentiment in whatever manner seems justified by the occasion, and helping to care for difficult situations that arise among small churches and upon missionary fields. For the most part now the pastors and the churches raise the missionary money themselves, and I am happy to say that they do it upon a much larger scale than I ever did it in the days of old. The State Board now asks the churches to set a goal which they will strive to reach in their offering. This is placing the responsibility upon the churches where it belongs. It has worked admirably. We have tried all the various systems that have been propagated and believe this to be the best. We used to make an apportionment, naming a sum ourselves which we thought the church ought to give. But this never did appeal to me as being either equitable to the churches or morally justified.

One of the former field duties of a Secretary was to hold meetings. The Secretary was the State Evangelist. It was during the last year of Billington's administration that the State Board voted the State Secretary out of the evangelistic field and gave him simply the secretary's work to do. They employed an evangelist to give his whole time to that type of work. Yet I have occasionally held meetings. Before the work of the Secretary became as heavy as it now is time could usually be found for one or two brief meetings each year. These would last all the way from a few nights in length to a month. In such manner I have held meetings at Baker, Mosier, Montavilla (Portland), Kern Park (Portland), Sellwood (Portland), Vernon (Portland), Canby, Talent, Newberg, Klamath Falls, Hillsboro, Estacada, and other places where the effort was not purely evangelistic. In one of the recent state conventions a resolution was presented making it obligatory upon the State Secretary to do evangelistic work for nine months in the year. The convention sensed the absurdity of such a proposal and voted it down so overwhelmingly that it has never come back.

A Secretary's field duties lead him to the organization of churches and setting in order weak and unstable ones. It was my privilege to open the way in Klamath Falls, Baker, Bend, Astoria, besides assisting in organization in many places where others had paved the way. At Bend after spying out the land I made regular monthly trips to care for the baby church until proper arrangements could be made for their care.

A Secretary is frequently called upon to help churches raise debts. This has been no inconsiderable part of my labors. Could I have commanded as much money for state missions as I have raised for local debts Oregon Missions would have been forging ahead at a great pace. While engaged in such an operation at Ashland one Sunday I noticed a visiting elder from a neighboring church sitting in the audience. He stayed all through the long, tedious appeal for money. When it was complete he arose and asked for the privilege of speaking. It was granted and he said: "I have known Brother Swander a long time, and have heard him ask for money many times; but this is the first time I ever heard him ask for money for anything except state missions, and I didn't know he could do it. I appreciate the fact that he does." The good brother just hadn't come in touch with that phase of my work. The facts are that I have raised more money for local churches than I have for State Missions.

Money raising is a joy when it is for God. I have seen the very heart of sacrifice laid bare in this work. I have seen men and women give until it actually hurt. Then I have seen others give when it hurt. There is a difference between giving *until* it hurts, and giving *when* it hurts. I have seen the miser draw his purse strings a little tighter and draw the knot a little harder. Yet I have never known a single one of God's people to come to want by reason of giving too much to the church. People's gifts are a correct index of their love for Christ and the Church. If they give much (proporionately so) it is because they love much. If they give little (proportionately so) it is because they love little. Where there is a will there is a way; and where people do not give it is because there is no will to give. Often, though, the will is greater than the gift. God will bless such gifts and such givers.

A Secretary is often called upon to settle difficulties within the membership. Perhaps it is to avert a division in the church; perhaps it is to heal up a division; perhaps it is to lead a disrupted church into the channels of harmony again. I have seen many church troubles and have helped to heal many. It is my conviction that there is no difficulty within the body that could not have been averted if all concerned had been wholly unselfish. The ambition to rule, the unwillingness to step out of a coveted position, the desire to foist upon others a certain method or doctrine—it is always something that places self above the cause. Lack of judgment, unwise procedure, tactless words and deeds have their full place in doing despite to God's house. But "woe unto him by whom the offence cometh."

Disciples of Christ are quite sensitive about "outside interference" in church matters. This sensitiveness particularly pertains in matters of church troubles. It is easy for a State Secretary, or any one else from outside a local church, to get "in bad" when dealing with such matters. Yet even orthodox disciples are not particularly opposed to any kind of interference so long as it is in their behalf. I have had calls from preachers to come over and help them—calls so camouflaged that one would never suspect their real intent, yet which proved in the end to be nothing more or less than a call to come and spank some obstreperous elder or deacon. I have had calls from elders and deacons which had but one purpose in view—to get rid of a preacher for them. Even disciples will submit to any kind of "dictation," "popery," "ecclesiasticism," or what not so long as it is in their personal favor. I have seen doughty knights of the cloth whip, vanquish, and slay an imaginary ecclesiastical foe; but when it was to their own interest they would lord it over God's heritage in a dictatorial manner that would put even the pope of Rome to shame. The author must confess to having his "eye teeth cut" as regards such matters in the early days of his secretaryship. Out of his experience he has evolved the iron clad rule that he will positively not enter into a local trouble except on invitation from the church or its official board. He will not knowingly respond to an appeal from a faction to meet with them, no matter whether the faction be right or wrong in his judgment. He is always willing to advise with anybody at any time; but in such cases as the above they must come to him instead of he going to them. He will go only on official invitation as cited above. He has found that this policy keeps him in the clear and permits him to go as a neutral instead of as the friend of a faction. If he goes on the invitation of a faction he loses caste immediately with the other faction.

Not infrequently is the Secretary called upon purely for counsel in matters pertaining to the local work. This is not because he knows more about it than they upon the field, nor because his judgment is superior to their own; but it is largely because the churches feel the need of a voice from the outside, some one who can look upon their matters in a dispassionate manner, some one who perhaps has known of other such experiences and can speak with a voice of certainty. Perhaps he will only confirm their own judgment, but that gives them confidence. Sometimes they want some one who will oppose present conditions when they themselves dare not take the initiative. It is a happy circumstance when a ''goat'' is handy. The Secretary often has to be the ''goat.''

The Secretary is frequently called upon for special occasions of various character. Perhaps they wish to dedicate a building and they desire to honor the Secretary. I have dedicated a number of buildings in the state— Mosier, Richland, Bend, Sellwood (Portland), Barlow, Corbett, Creswell, Klamath Falls, Bridge, Grants Pass, Lexington, Lostine, Wallowa. Perhaps they desire to set aside some of their young people to the ministry—it has been my joy to assist in a number of such occasions. Perhaps they desire to ordain, or install, church officers— this has always been a pleasant function. Perhaps it is an annual meeting—some churches make annual reservation for such date. Perhaps it is only a reception of some kind—it is always good to be present on these gracious social occasions where the ladies usually preside, at least actually, if not formally so. Whatever the function the Secretary must respond as graciously as he does to any other demand. Happy is the Secretary who is called upon for such functions! It denotes that his people love him, have confidence in him, and wish to honor him.

In the preparation for conventions the Secretary is expected to take a prominent part. While there is a committee for making the program for state conventions, yet the Secretary must attend those meetings, keep a record of them, and do the correspondence incident to them. The information that is necessary to the making of these programs must be furnished by him and must be on the tip of his tongue. If there be district, or county, conventions he is usually invited to attend and to take part on the program. I have even had local committees ask me to just attend to the making of the program.

In the State Board organization the Secretary is an important factor. He must make a detailed report at each meeting, which happens to be four times each year in Oregon. He must make a written report to the annual convention. He must have a docket of necessary items that must be cared for by the Board and keeps a record of their actions. He is a member of all the standing committees appointed by the Board, and upon him depends largely the functioning of these committees.

One of the sad features of a Secretary's work is concerning unworthy men in the ministry. There is no body of men in all the world that is so clean as a whole as the Christian ministry. Yet occasionally a "man of the cloth" does wrong—not simply a misstep, nor unwittingly, but he commits sin of such character that his brethren cannot overlook it. There is no man in the world who is watched with such eagle eye as the preacher. If he oversteps the bounds of propriety even by a small margin Dame Gossip is ready to mouth his name with all sorts of unclean rumors. It has been my policy to disregard unsupported rumors about preachers, and to stand by them until tangible evidence is brought indisputably into the clear that involves them in wrongdoing. In a number of cases I have thus stood by men for several years while reports kept coming about them. I have admonished men to be careful and to avoid even the "appearance of evil" that their names be not brought into disrepute. When charges are brought to me involving the good name of a brother minister I endeavor first of all to get those charges defined in definite cases, and put in writing if possible. They are then reported to the State Board. The Board usually appoints a committee to investigate the case. The committee sifts all the evidence possible to get and pronounces its convictions accordingly. The exact procedure is determined by the individual setting of each case. No iron clad rule is followed. If the man is found guilty of a gravely wrong act, from which he has not repented the committee recommends that he no longer be recognized on our roll of ministers. That is the extreme penalty that can be inflicted acccording to our church polity. If the act of which he has been found guilty is only an indiscretion of conduct he is admonished as a brother and advised to be more circumspect in the future. If there be found no evidence of his guilt the committee so declares. The committee's action has always been considered final. In a few notorious and especially aggravated cases the State Board has taken an action without appointing a committee. But the State Board is not an ecclesiastical court; and, where the sifting of evidence is required, it will not assume the function of a court. The Board will serve simply as a clearing house through which these matters may be dealt with in justice to the accused and to the honor of the church. Many cases in the last twenty years have been thus dealt with. The Secretary is usually made the "goat" for the committee's action and on more than one occasion has the wrath of man been visited upon his head because of action

taken as above outlined. He personally, and the State
Board corporately, have been threatened with all kinds
of vengeance because of such attitudes toward sin. The
minister who sins is not to be shielded in his sin. If the
ministry is not willing to condemn sin when it is found in
its own ranks how can we expect the courts of Caesar to
mete out justice to Caesar's minions!

The Secretary meets with many personal experiences in
the course of his ministry—some of which are laughable,
some of which are sad, and some of which are serious.
It would take a volume to relate them, but a few will be
inserted here to add a bit of flavor to the chapter.

One feature that is a never ending wonderment of "what
is next" is the beds he sleeps in. Once in a personal letter
to a friend, written just after such an "experience" I
remarked that I was seriously thinking of writing a book
and entitling it "Beds I Have Slept In." No one knows
better how prolific of interest such a theme would be. For
the most part the Secretary is entertained in the homes of
the brethren. Let it be said right here that 99 per cent
of the beds he sleeps in are 100 per cent good. It is the
other 1 per cent that creates the diversion. And the experiences are not all with beds in homes, either; many of
them are in hotels.

I was taken to a farm home one night after meeting.
It was a humble home, but the folks were upright, Christian people. The bedroom was of the "spare" variety.
It was small, not larger than eight by ten feet, and was
used generally as a storeroom for a variety of stuff.
Neither its size, nor its contents, were objectionable: but
the window—the one lone window—was nailed down. Try
as hard as I could it would not budge. I arose in the

morning with a feeling like "the morning after." That
night in a small room, with no ventilation, cost the work
a whole day of time, for I was wholly unfit for work of
any description the next day. It should be remarked here,
lest this recital be interpreted as derogatory to the farmer,
that this same experience was repeated in a town of 6,000
population, only the room was about six times as large
and the ill effects were not so marked.

Sometimes psychology has a good deal to do with our
experiences. I was in a railroad berth one night where
one has less than a hundred cubic feet of air to breathe.
I very carefully opened the window and felt the cool screen
just beyond. I would be breathing pure, fresh air from
outdoors all night long! I slept as sweetly as a babe,
and felt as fine as possible upon awakening the next morning. But I was considerably disconcerted a little later to
discover that just beyond the screen I had felt was another
window shut as tight as a water cask. After all imagination may have something to do with our ills, and that is
the kernel of Christian Science (so called).

The Secretary was obliged to detrain one dark night
about 2 o'clock at a country crossing and wait for a branch
train some time next morning. Stepping off the train I
saw nothing in sight that looked like a town—nothing in
sight but the depot and switch lights. Upon inquiring
of the brakeman I was told to go down the track to a certain switch light, turn to the left and go up a hill. I
would find a hotel up there. I did as directed and found
a large, rambling frame structure with a porch across the
front. It was dark without and pitch dark within, and
there was no sign by which I could identify the entrances.
I tried a door, but it was locked. I pounded on it but no

one responded. I finally gave up in disgust and was planning to return to the depot and seek a couch upon a bench *a la hobo.* Just then a man came up the hill who told me he could get me in the hotel, and he did. He took me up to a room that was cold, the linen on the bed worn and dirty, a cracked bowl and a pitcher of dirty water, a traditional rickety chair—that comprised the furnishings. There was that suspicious feeling all the time that something was crawling. Heavy eyed and weary I wended my way downstairs with the first sign of dawn. I had prepared myself for the worst yet—breakfast. But *mirabile dictu!* A more appetizing meal of hot cakes, syrup, cured ham and coffee I never sat down to! I left that place with the feeling that "all's well that ends well." It may be agreeable to Oregon disciples to know that this incident occurred in a neighboring state instead of our own.

Two other hotel experiences are here called to mind. There is a certain town (name withheld, but in Oregon) into which it has frequently been my lot to arrive in the middle of the night. On the first occasion I inquired of the agent for a hotel and he directed me "two blocks up and a block over, then up a flight of stairs." I finally located the place and it was a typical "last chance." It consisted of the half of a bed (not a half-bed), the other half of which was occupied. The bed was dirty and the occupant was even dirtier. It was a toss-up between buying that bed space and camping out under the stars with only the heavens for a canopy. The night was cold and the bed space won—dirt and all. The aftermath lasted several days—I was that long getting rid of little friends that were determined to stick closer than a brother.

The other incident happened in the same town several

years later. This time the town had three fairly respectable hotels and I did not anticipate the same experience as before. Nor did I find it. Two travelling men got off the same train with me. The three of us went to the best hotel—and found every bed full. Together we went to the second best—result, the same. Together we went to the third, and last, place, and oh! Joy! There were two vacant beds there! One of the travelling men was very agile in saying, "I'll take one." The other travelling man looked at me and unselfishly said, "You take the other one." I looked him up and down and replied, "I'll share it with you." When once up in the room we introduced ourselves. He asked me my business and I told him I was a minister of the Christian Church. He then told me his religion—he was a Roman Catholic. Notwithstanding his religion I slept soundly. The next morning he told me confidentially how I could beat the restaurant for a part of my breakfast. I thanked him gratefully, but did not use the information.

A similar experience at a Junction point one night turned out more agreeably. After agreeing to share a room with a stranger it turned out that he was a Methodist preacher going out to take up his first circuit. I decided that if I didn't look any more like a preacher than he did I would be perfectly safe anywhere.

A more serious experience with beds occurred in a little Oregon town one night in midwinter. I arrived in the place late in the evening and a stopping place among the brethren did not materialize. I went to the hotel which was dark. The landlord responded to a call by telling me to go in the bedroom off the parlor and help myself. Groping my way through the dark I finally located a drop

light by swinging my arms in circles, and finally discovered
the bedroom. It was the typical "spare bed," and it had
evidently been "spared" occupancy a long time. No fire
had ever disgraced that room. The sheets were cold and
clammy. I left on as much clothing as decency would
allow and turned in. The hospitality was paid for by a
kind elder, but I paid the heavier price with a cold that
I did not get rid of for many weeks.

Another "spare" bed was in a public rooming house in
a town of 7,000 population. It was so cold that I got up
in the night and took the rug off the floor for a covering.
Failing in that to keep warm I built a fire in the stove
with the scanty fuel that was there in an effort to ward
off disease germs that affect the tissues of the lungs and
throat.

There have been some beautiful experiences that are in
marked contrast with those just related. Peregrinating
over the state as a Secretary must I have been impressed
with the beauties of nature which God has scattered so
lavishly on every hand in Oregon. Whether it is along
the Columbia river with its perpendicular walls of solid
rock on the one hand and "where rolls the Oregon" on
the other; or whether it is along the Des Chutes with its
series of rapids between banks of flaming color; or whether
it is through desert fields peopled only with the aromatic
sage or the pungent juniper; or whether it is through the
mountains cut and slashed with deep gorges, or set with
emerald lakes, or decorated with stately firs; or whether
it is through the cultivated lands with their varied crops;
it is all the same—an unending splendor of glory. Coming down the Columbia river one day I was attracted to
a gentleman occupying the seat just ahead of me who was

going into raptures over the scenery through which we
were passing. I spoke to him and asked him whence he
came. He replied that for twenty-five years he had been
a Baptist missionary on the Congo in Africa; that he had
counted the Congo the most beautiful river in the world,
and he had travelled around the globe; but he had never
seen anything so beautiful in all his travels as the Columbia river scenery. How true it is that those living in the
midst of beauty often fail to see it! It is also very sad.

It is a never failing source of joy to ride through the
mountains of Southern Oregon along the way of the
Southern Pacific Railroad. Cow Creek Canyon has only
one defect—its name. Wolf Creek Canyon may be rightly
named, but the name cannot hint the beauty of its course.
One looks at a painted picture and accuses the artist of
exaggerating the color; but after looking once at the placid
blue of Crater Lake, or upon the flaming colors of the rocks
in the Des Chutes Canyon, or upon the lights and shadows
that play upon the many snow capped peaks, he must
confess that "the half has not been told," even by the
artist.

My first trip into Coos county was by the old-fashioned
four-horse stage over the old Coos Bay road which leaves
Roseburg, through beautiful Looking Glass Valley, and
finally comes to an abrupt end at Sumner on an arm of
Coos Bay. The trip through the valley was not so pleasant
because of the heat and the dust. But by nightfall we had
passed out of the heat and the dust and had entered the
mountain passes. After stopping for supper at a wayside
inn it was my good fortune to draw a seat in the boot with
the driver for the remainder of the journey. About 11
o'clock the moon arose in all her dignity. From then until

12 o'clock midnight we were passing through dense forest—tall and towering firs, black walls of solid rock first on one hand and then on the other, the moonbeams playing hide-and-seek between the masses of green boughs and popping out suddenly from behind masses of rock, its shadows and beams like grey ghosts flickering before the vision. The driver spared not his steeds, keeping them on the gallop where the grade permitted, swinging around sharp curves until screams of fright came from the passengers, punctuating it all with stories of holdups and upsets until one was ready to jump at a moment's notice. Finally we landed at Sumner and the passengers were put on a little gasoline launch and were taken to Marshfield. I was asleep when we landed and was ready for bed again when we were finally ushered into the old Blanco Hotel at 2 o'clock in the morning. I have never had occasion to go over that road since, but that moonlight drive will always linger in my memory as one of the beautiful things I have seen. I have had many trips since with the four-horse stage, but that is a thing of the past now. A modern pavement and automobile takes one into Coos county now in 3 hours as against 19 in that olden day.

In Wheeler county, on the road from Fossil to Spray, the trail (for it was nothing more than a trail when I first traversed it) led through a dense forest of red pine trees. There was no sign of underbrush and the trees were sufficiently spaced to leave the impression of an artificial park. Many trees were three feet in diameter and one could not help but think of the majesty of the Creator that would provide such a beautiful earth for human delectation. It was on that trip we stopped at a halfway house for dinner. While the other passengers took lunch in the farm kitchen

I took mine on the sunny side of a haystack from a lunch box which my good hostess of the night before had thoughtfully provided. The other passengers were inclined to jest at my expense, telling me I didn't know what I had missed. And I didn't, thank God! I discovered what it was, though, on the return trip. If flies had been kept for breeding purposes there couldn't have been more on that table. I had not supposed there were so many flies in the whole world. I cheerfully paid my fifty cents for the privilege of escaping from that kitchen table rather than for the dinner, for I could not eat.

Speaking of flies I am just reminded of a railroad stop on a new branch road somewhere in Oregon. It was just a lunch counter, evidently run with little profit, and probably only for the convenience of train passengers, for there was no other population near. There were some delicious looking ham sandwiches on the counter. I ate one with great relish and wanted more. I took a huge bite out of the second one and ate it. Just then my eye caught sight of the mustard jar and I decided upon an appetizer. I opened the sandwich to spread the mustard, and—before my eyes there lay stiff and cold in death a huge house fly. My appetite was suddenly satisfied. I grew sick at the stomach. I picked up the sandwich and walked over to the cashier, spread it out before him and said as politely as I could, "Here's your sandwich, Mister. How much do you want for it?" He picked it up quickly, tossed it under the counter, and bade me pass on. That was my first and only time to ever receive a pass at the lunch counter.

Returning to the subject of drives there is an automobile ride that will always stand out in my memory for having produced the sensation of fright within me. It was on a trip in a private car (beg pardon, it was a Ford) from Fort Rock, in Lake county, to Bend, a distance of some seventy miles. We left Fort Rock about 6 o'clock in the evening. For a considerable distance we travelled through the sage brush country without anything more exciting than a tire puncture which was easily mended. When night had fairly fallen around us we were in the tall timber. It was a beautiful drive through the timber with the trail winding in and out among the tall trees. I was sitting with the driver. For a time a desultory conversation had been carried on. Finally I grew drowsy, and was just about yielding myself to a siesta, when I sat up wide-awake. A thought had entered my mind, and with it the cold perspiration stood out on my brow. The thought that struck me was this, "What if the driver should drop asleep?" I spoke to him. He answered promptly, but immediately stopped the car and got out. He raised the hood of the engine and seemed to tinker with the mechanism for a few moments. Finally he got back in the car and we started up again. "Anything wrong?" I queried. "Nothing," he replied, "Only when you spoke I was asleep and I just got out to wake up." Needless to say conversation did not lag during the rest of the journey.

An embarrassing and humorous situation was created by trying to be "smart" one day. I was touring the state holding missionary rallies in company with W. F. Turner, C. E. Benlehr from India, and Mrs. Eda T. Moore from St. Louis. The rallies included luncheon at the church both noon and evening. Almost every place we went the menu included potato salad. After about three weeks of potato salad it was a bit ruffling to the temper to even look a potato in the eye. At one place the ladies had a delicious hot dinner prepared. It was so appetizing that we all ate heartily. The "team" wanted me to express their appreciation of this very fine courtesy, which I did in the best chosen words I could command. I thought to close my words with a facetious remark, and said: "And you are to be particularly congratulated for being able to serve so good a dinner without having potato salad." One of the ladies who was serving spoke up immediately and said, "Oh, Brother Swander, we are going to have the potato salad tonight." The laugh was on me and it was exceedingly hearty. I had long before learned that there are times when silence is golden. I decided that this was one of them.

During the earlier part of my secretaryship I was taught a lesson in humility by a veteran of the cross in such a manner that I have never forgotten it. L. N. Judd, nearly a nonegenarian in age, lived in Ashland. He was one of the old time preachers. I had called on him once when he was sick, thus gaining favor with him until he passed over. A conference of the churches in Jackson county was being held at Phoenix one summer. A bower of branches was built for the meetings and some of the brethren camped during the short time the conference lasted. Brother Judd was one of them. I was to speak at a certain hour and my shoes were quite dusty and unfit to appear on the platform. Seeing that Brother Judd's shoes were always immaculately clean I suspected that he had a shoe brush with him, and made bold to ask if I might borrow it. "Oh, yes, yes," he replied, and immediately ran to get it. But instead of "loaning" it to me as I had asked he said. "I am going to have the honor of brushing your shoes for you.'' I protested that I could not permit so old a man to brush the shoes of so young a man, but all in vain. Very simply and humbly he said, ''My Saviour washed his disciples' feet and said to them, 'I have given you an example, that ye also should do as I have done unto you.' This is the nearest I can come to following my Master's example, and I want to be like him.'' I saw that this saint of God meant it. It would hurt him to be refused his way and so I permitted him to do it. But it taught me a great lesson. The world will never know the feeling of shortcoming that surged through my soul while this aged disciple of Christ was cleaning my shoes.

During the first six years of my secretaryship there was a splendid little country church at the little crossroads community of Bridge, in Coos county. The church had been started in an ''upper room'' in the home of Brother and Sister A. L. Nosler. Later a church house was built. I came to entertain a very strong personal affection for these brethren and took great pleasure in spending a few days vacation with them in the summer time. George E. Williams, who was our state evangelist, likewise shared a fraternal feeling for them, and it was our greatest sport to spend a few days in these hills shooting ''diggers.'' For the sake of the uninitiated I will say that a ''digger'' is a beautiful, little grey squirrel that derived its name from the fact that it dug for its home a hole in the ground. These squirrels had a habit of sitting on their haunches right at the edge of the hole. It was a chance shot that bagged one of these little creatures. Even though hit and mortally wounded the chances were that they would fall back into the hole and disappear from view, leaving the hunter to imagine whether or not he had killed his prey.

In true hunter style we usually counted him in the toll for the day. The brethren were not at all averse to accompany us on these incursions. The hills would echo back and forth with the explosion of shells like the bursting of artillery. A little while of this and the diggers would all be frightened into their homes for that day and we would have to move on to another field. The farmers were glad to have the little animals slaughtered for they did much damage to the crops. These Coos county vacations were among the best of my life.

The office of State Secretary does not carry as many perquisites with it as the pastorate. Weddings are few, though there are some special friendships that call for him on that occasion. Funerals are more numerous. As a rule a small gratuity is attached to these. One man whose wife's funeral I had conducted called me into the home after the service and literally emptied his pockets of paper and silver money, thrusting it into my hands and would not take a refusal. Special addresses have sometimes brought in a small perquisite. But the perquisites in money would not swell the income of the secretary very much. There have been gifts other than money that have touched my heart very deeply. Just before Christmas one year I was with a little church, and after service had dropped into a drug store with my host where I waited while he was making some purchases. While waiting I was looking at the display of Christmas goods and my eye fell upon a leather toilet case. I took it off the table and opened it up. It appeared to be the most complete, and most compact, case I had ever seen. I suppose my eyes must have betrayed my pleasure with it, and perhaps I looked upon it longer than I should. I was aroused by a voice just behind me, "Would you like to have that?" Without intending to indicate more than a gratification with the article I replied in the affirmative. "Take it along as a Christmas present from me," he said. I protested, but he insisted. That case has travelled with me many thousand miles.

One year my wife's birthday was coming on apace. I had decided on getting her a genuine Indian blanket for a present. Thinking it would please her a bit more if I purchased it direct from the factory I wrote to H. H. Hubbell, then pastor of the church at Pendleton, and asked him to get a pretty one for me and bring it down to the State Board meeting that would be held just prior to the birth date. He did so, and when I asked him for the price that I might pay him, he replied: "This is a present from the Pendleton church. They appreciate you and the work you are doing, and they wanted to show it by furnishing this robe for you." It was a forceful reminder that a man's compensation consisteth not alone in his salary. That robe still graces the lounge in our home and will continue to do so as long as there is a home to be graced, or until the robe is worn out in gracing the home. My wife has never been quite certain whether I gave her the birthday present that year or not. She is inclined to doubt it.

The Klamath Falls brethren have shown their appreciation of the State Secretary in various ways. It was my privilege to assist them in raising a $4,000 debt on their basement. At the close of the service that night the chairman of their board walked to the front and in a few well chosen words he expressed the appreciation of the church for the services rendered, and closed by presenting me with a full leather suit case from the Board of Officers. The next morning the treasurer was to hand me a check for the expenses of my trip. To my surprise it exceeded the amount of expense I had handed in, and supposing he had made a mistake I called his attention to it. "No," he said, "That is all right. The Board instructed me to write in $25.00 for you personally." Before getting out of town, C. F. Stemwell, a clothier of the city and now of sainted memory, called me into his store and told me to pick out any shirt and tie in the establishment as a token of his personal appreciation of my services to the church. These things mean much more than the monetary value of them, and they serve to offset the many discouraging experiences that make a man wonder sometimes if it is worthwhile to persevere. We know that it is.

In addition to these things one could mention many more. I dare not attempt to mention the names of donors lest the memory prove faulty, but in the matter of gifts there have been found canned and smoked salmon, apples, peaches, pears, cherries, canned fruit, raisins, prunes, dried venison, books, clothing, candies, and many other things. In so many ways have people shown their appreciation that it would be impossible to give credit to all. But appreciation for it all lives in the heart continually.

In closing I wish to relate what has been one of the most touching incidents in all this ministry. Up in the hills back from Talent there lived an aged couple who were both in their eighties. The husband was a veritable patriarch with his flowing grey beard. The wife was a wonderfully sweet faced little old lady, and she was stone blind. The old man had a "mine" which he worked industriously and in the constant expectation that he would strike it rich, then he could provide suitably for his loved companion. She, dear old soul, encouraged him faithfully. In company with Brother and Sister W. L. Mellinger, from Ashland, Mrs. Frank Guisinger, from Talent, and Mrs. Nannie Stevenson, from Portland, I called upon Brother and Sister Cain. We talked and prayed with them, and Mrs. Stevenson sang the songs of Zion for them. It was a mountain top experience, both physically and spiritually. The old peoples' faces actually shone as we prayed and sang together. We wended our way back to town with a certainty made still more certain that the life in Christ Jesus is something more than the physical life we live here for three score years and ten, more or less. Brother and Sister Cain have passed over by this time. But the day spent in that humble mountain cabin was worth more to me than the richer hospitality in a mansion where Christ is not known. Believing that our work of spreading abroad the gospel in Oregon is helping to enlarge the number of homes where Christ dwells we cannot help but feel that it has been worth while; and we indulge the hope that when we shall all meet over there, and where we "shall know as we are known," that we may be permitted to have visualized the product of these years as State Secretary of Oregon.

TABLE OF OFFERINGS
Oregon Missionary Purposes

Year	Churches	B. S.	C. E.	Con. Exp.	Prop'ty	Permanent	Special
1878	$ 449.25	$	$	$	$	$	$
1880	134.25						
1881	67.45						
1882	174.45						
1883	309.95						
1891	240.75		5.00				
1899	711.69	20.25	5.00	254.90			
1900	667.85	25.00		26.90			
1901	543.23	35.00	24.57	245.10			19.10
1902	941.38	55.72	56.50	442.23			37.75
1906	2,017.23						
1907	1,334.81						93.65
1908	2,244.68				893.86		
1909	1,890.32						
1910	3,127.78			78.00	489.82		436.50
1911	2,917.72			146.43	87.00		
1912	3,364.33						14.11
1913	3,978.66			91.10	231.86		
1914	2,252.12		25.00	92.85			
1915	2,881.42			104.31			
1916	2,848.70	399.25	20.00	133.40			
1917	2,332.77	484.24		117.60			
1918	2,448.18	662.37				50.00	1,500.00
1919	4,844.61	451.43		111.85		575.31	
1920	5,081.18	719.32		93.50		1,017.32	34.84
1921	5,900.00	1,225.23	78.00	204.30	20.00	667.22	749.35
1922	4,987.51	1,123.31		222.51	490.10	500.96	
1923	5,277.97	1,082.16		281.67	653.03	53 00	220.81
1924	6,158.97	976.10	25.00	305.63	41.00	20.00	40.00
1925	6,464.70	1,099.80	147.84	458.77		10.00	271.40
1926	7,221.56	1,030.41	50.00	244.07		119.96	4.70
1927	6,300.73	1,164.80	26.75	400.19			
1928	6,004.18	1,204.83	8.75	452.21		80.00	161.50
	$96,120.38	$11,759.22	$472.41	$4,507.52	$2,906.67	$3,093.77	$3,583.71

OFFICIAL DIRECTORY

Date Convention	Held at	President	Secretary
1852	McCoy	Glen O. Burnett	-------------
1853	Rickreal(?)	-------------	-------------
1854	Luckimute(?)	-------------	-------------
1855	----------	-------------	-------------
1856	----------	-------------	-------------
1857, September	----------	-------------	-------------
1858, September	Mill Creek	-------------	-------------
1859, August	Monmouth	-------------	-------------

The Christian Missionary Society of Oregon

Date Convention	Held at	President	Secretary
1860, Sept. 7	Eola	Jas. R. Fisher	Wm. Porter
1861, September	Silver Creek	-------------	-------------
1862	Bethany(?)	-------------	-------------
1863, June	Eola	-------------	-------------
1863, October	Central	John E. Murphey	Reuben Doty
1863, December	Monmouth	-------------	-------------
1864, June	McMinnville	-------------	-------------
1865, June 25	Bethel	-------------	-------------
1866	----------	-------------	-------------
1867	----------	-------------	-------------
1868	Monmouth	-------------	-------------
1869	LaCreole (Rickreal)	-------------	-------------
1870	La Creole	-------------	-------------
1871	La Creole	-------------	-------------
1872	La Creole	-------------	-------------
1873	La Creole	-------------	-------------
1874	Dixie (Rickreal)	-------------	-------------
1875	Dixie	-------------	-------------
1876	Dixie	-------------	-------------
1877, June	Dallas	-------------	B. Wolverton

The Annual State Cooperation

Date Convention	Held at	President	Secretary
1878, November	Monmouth	-------------	S. C. Adams
1879, Nov. 4	Monmouth	Bruce Wolverton	S. C. Adams
1880, Nov. 9	Portland	J. W. Cowls	S. C. Adams
1881, Nov. 8-11	Amity	-------------	S. C. Adams
1882, Oct. 18-21	Eugene	W. H. Adams	B. Wolverton
1883, Oct. 3-6	Salem	W. H. Adams	J. W. Spriggs
1884, June	Portland	-------------	-------------
1885, June	Turner	-------------	-------------
1886, June	Turner	-------------	-------------
1887, June	Turner	-------------	-------------
1888, June	Turner	D. M. Doty	P. R. Burnett
1889, June	Turner	-------------	P. R. Burnett

The Christian Missionary Convention of Oregon, Inc.

Date Convention	Held at	President	Secretary
1890, June	Turner	_____	J. F. Stewart
1891, June 22-27	Turner	David Wetzel	J. F. Stewart
1892, June	Turner	C. A. Shelbrede	B. F. Mulkey
1893, June 15-25	Turner	C. A. Shelbrede	B. F. Mulkey*
1894, June	Turner	W. H. Hawley	J. B. Lister
1895, June	Turner	W. H. Osborne	J. B. Lister
1896, June	Turner	W. H. Osborne	J. B. Lister
1897, June	Turner	K. H. Sickafoose	J. B. Lister
1898, June	Turner	Morton L. Rose	J. B. Lister
1899, Jun.23-Jul.3	Turner	Morton L. Rose	J. B. Lister
1900, Jun.22-Jul.2	Turner	Morton L. Rose	J. B. Lister
1901, Jun.21-Jul.1	Turner	Morton L. Rose	J. B. Lister
1902, June 20-30	Turner	Albyn Esson	J. B. Lister
1903, June	Turner	Albyn Esson	J. B. Lister
1904, June	Turner	J. S. McCallum	J. J. Evans
1905, June	Turner	J. W. Jenkins	F. E. Billington
1906, Jun.21-Jul.1	Turner	J. W. Jenkins	F. E. Billington
1907, June 20-30	Turner	Davis Errett	F. E. Billington
1908, Jun.22-Jul.5	Turner	Davis Errett	C. F. Swander
1909, Jun.24-Jul.2	Turner	Davis Errett	C. F. Swander
1910, Jun.25-Jul.3	Turner	Davis Errett	C. F. Swander
1911, July 1-4	Portland	Albyn Esson	C. F. Swander

The Oregon Christian Missionary Convention

1912, June 22-30	Turner	Albyn Esson	C. F. Swander
1913, June 19-29	Turner	Albyn Esson	C. F. Swander
1914, July 8-16	Turner	Albyn Esson	C. F. Swander
1915, July 6-14	Turner	Albyn Esson	C. F. Swander
1916, July 8-16	Turner	Albyn Esson	C. F. Swander
1917, Jul.28-Ag.5	Turner	F. T. Porter	C. F. Swander
1918, July 6-14	Turner	F. T. Porter†	C. F. Swander
1919, July 5-13	Turner	E. V. Stivers	C. F. Swander
1920, July 3-11	Turner	E. V. Stivers	C. F. Swander
1921, July 2-10	Turner	E. V. Stivers	C. F. Swander
1922, July 1-9	Turner	E. V. Stivers	C. F. Swander
1923, Jun.30-Jul.8	Turner	E. V. Stivers	C. F. Swander
1924, July 5-13	Turner	E. V. Stivers	C. F. Swander
1925, Jun.27-Jul.5	Turner	E. V. Stivers	C. F. Swander
1926, July 3-11	Turner	E. V. Stivers	C. F. Swander
1927, July 2-10	Turner	E. V. Stivers	C. F. Swander
1928, Jun.30-Jul.8	Turner	E. V. Stivers	C. F. Swander

*The records show that in the year 1893-94 L. F. Stephens served the last 4 months instead of B. F. Mulkey.

†In the year 1918-19 A. L. Crim succeeded F. T. Porter as President when the latter entered war service.

MINISTERS WHO HAVE LABORED IN THE STATE OF OREGON

Great pains have been taken to make this list complete and accurate. Many records have been searched for names, yet it is more than likely that some have eluded search. But this is a worthy list, and we shall be glad for any correction thereto.

A

Adams, Andrew J.
Adams, Sebastian
Adams, William L.
Adams, W. T.
Alexander, John M.
Allison, Virgil K.
Ames, E. O.
Andrews, Frank A.
Applebury, T. R.
Applegate, J. Merle
Arant, Francis M.
Armstrong, J. A.
Ashley, J. Francis
Atchley, E. F.

B

Bailes, Ira
Bailey, L. Y.
Bailey, S. Y.
Baird, William R.
Baker, A. D.
Ball, H. H.
Ball, J. W.
Barkley, J. H.
Barnes, E. W.
Barney, William V.
Bass, B. W.
Bass, H. J.
Bates, Arthur C.

Beach, Nathan E.
Bean, William E.
Beattie, James A.
Beaudreau, E. F.
Beery, Archer A.
Bell, Harry
Bell, H. L.
Bennett, Abe F.
Bennett, James A.
Bennett, J. C.
Bennett, W. J.
Benny, Chris J.
Benny, Louis H.
Benton, Harry
Benton, H. E.
Benton, Mary D.
Berry, George K.
Biggs, J. Quincy
Billington, Frank E.
Black, B. C.
Blanchard, W. W.
Bobbitt, W. E.
Bogue, Jasper
Bond, Stanley N.
Bonnell, B. F.
Boulten, Clarence A.
Bower, Clark
Blessing, William L.
Bower, Milton W.
Boyd, Joseph D.
Boyle, D. D.

Bradshaw, Charles
Bridges, Jonathan
Briggs, Samuel
Bristow, Arlo B.
Bristow, Elijah
Brooke, Frederick M.
Brooks, N. H.
Brown, Judson
Brown, T. F.
Browning, E. G.
Browning, Nelson L.
Brownrigg, M.
Brunk, Alfred
Brunk, Hugh D.
Buchanan, Amos
Burch, E. L.
Burke, Kendall E.
Burnett, Glen O.
Burnett, Peter R.
Burr, Eugene
Burris, Oliver P.
Burton, B. B.
Burton, C. J.
Burton, Walter
Bussabarger, R. Lee

C

Callison, Gilmore
Callison, Rufus G.
Calliso, Walter
Campbell, James A.
Campbell, Prince L.
Campbell, T. F.
Cannon, T. J.
Cane, Arthur
Carey, Clifford L.
Carlson, J. Eric
Carson, Amy (Phillips)
Cartwright, R. L.
Cash, Ashley B.
Casteel, Elder
Caswell, J. C.
Chamlee, Lon I.
Champie, Henry S.
Champie, Josephine (Patterson)
Chandler, Earl C.
Chapman, ———

Chase, W. F.
Cheetham, Neal
Child, E. A.
Childers, S. Earl
Childers, T. L.
Clark, H. Campbell
Clay, Benjamin Frank!:
Coker, Robert H.
Coley, Fred
Comstock, Clark W.
Conder, John Perry
Confer, Earl P.
Conner, Samuel M.
Cook, Francis L.
Cooper, Oscar A.
Copple, Robert A.
Corbin, A. C.
Coultard, J. H.
Coulter, E. E.
Crane, W. A.
Crawford, J. V.
Crawford, E. I.
Crediford, D. Royce
Crim, A. L.
Crockatt, Peter
Crockett, Walter Scott
Crow, Ben C.
Cunningham, J. Frank
Cupp, Louis S.
Curtis, Charles C.
Curtis, Oliver L.

D

Dallas, Rex R.
Darby, Oliver E.
Davidson, Elijah B.
Deming, W. L.
Dent, Dorsey
Denton, H. A.
Diggins, W. A.
Dodd, A. H.
Dorris, Victor
Doty, D. M.
Doty, R.
Dotson, C. A.
Doward, Z. O.
Downing, Earl F.

Drake, Charles R.
Drill, Guy L.
Duffy, George F.
Dunn, C. V.
Dunn, Roy L.
Dunton, Ted

E

Easter, J. P.
Eaton, Arthur T.
Eaton, A. C.
Ellett, Lertis R.
Elder, A. R.
Elkins, Willard A.
Elliott, Luke D.
Elliott, Stephen
Ellis, Ford
Emerich, J. Albert
Emerson, F. A.
Emerson, Frank W.
Emery, Guy
Emmons, E. J.
Erickson, A.
Errett, Davis
Esson, Albyn
Esson, Mrs. Clara G.
Evans, John J.
Evans, S. D.

F

Fagan, M. Howard
Farrow, Eugene O.
Ferguson, Lee
Fesler, C. L.
Fisher, Eli
Fisher, James R.
Fishback, Len B.
Fite, J. Raymond
Fleshman, O. C.
Flinn, E. M.
Floyd, J. F.
Ford, Harry L.
Ford, Palmer
Forell, E. von
Foster, Hugh
Foster, John
Friend, W. G.

G

Gardner, Arthur E.
Garinger, John J.
Gervin, J. H.
Ghormley, J. Carlos
Ghormley, J. F.
Gillum, E. W.
Gilstrap, Elmore J.
Gist, O. J.
Givens, Walter
Glasscock, S. W.
Goodwin, A. Ted
Gordon, A. C. Duff
Grant, S. P.
Green, Leon D.
Gregg, Samuel
Gressman, William A.
Griffis, Harold H.
Guiley, Ross
Gwinn, H. B.

H

Hackett, Dwight W.
Hale, J. Willis
Haley, W. T.
Hall, Maxwell
Hanhy, A. J.
Hamm, F. Grant
Handsaker, John J.
Handsaker, Thomas S.
Hanna, J. C.
Hanson, C.
Harding, Mary C.
Hargus, Oliver
Harlan, S. D.
Harmon, J. H.
Harness, George N.
Harriman, Arthur A.
Harriman, Dickson P.
Harriman, Fred E.
Harris, Ellis B.
Harris, O. D.
Harris, John M.
Hartley, A. C.
Harvey, Amos
Harvey, Guy R.
Hawk, Jeu

Hawkins, Samuel R.
Hay, Garland W.
Hayes, Willard
Hazel, I. H.
Healy, Roy
Helseth, Emil
Hendricks, Kenneth
Hendricks, Russell
Hendrix _____
Hervey, A. E.
Hicks, B. L.
Hilton, Charles H.
Hoag, J. B.
Hohgatt, Cyrus Hersell
Hollenbeck, S. B.
Hollingsworth, Austin J.
Holmes, J. B.
Hopkins, C. Homer
Horn, Marion F.
Hoskin, L. E.
Hoven, Ard
Hoven, Victor E.
Hovrud, Oscar
Howe, D. J.
Hubbell, Harvey H.
Huffman, H. H.
Hug, Ray
Hugh, Louie
Hull, Harold
Humbert, G. S. O.
Humbert, Harold F.
Hunter, J. M.
Huntington _____
Husband, David
Husby, Kenneth J.
Hutchins, Howard
Hutton, Glen W.
Hypes, Gordon

I

Iler, H. B.
Ingram, W. D.
Irons, S.
Isaacson, Ralph
Isaacson, Roy S.

J

Jackson, S. W.
Jameson, R. F.
Jenkins, J. W.
Jessup, William
Johnson, Charles Wesley
Johnson, George F. G.
Johnson, J. R.
Johnson, Norman
Johnson, R. L.
Jones, E. E.
Jones, Frank E.
Jones, Herbert F.
Jones, Lester I.
Jones, O. W.
Jones, S. A.
Jones, T. M.
Jones, Wallace E.
Jope, R. E.
Jordan, Elmer W.
Jordan, Galen E.
Judd, L. N.

K

Kellems, David C.
Kellems, Homer
Kellems, Jesse R.
Kellems, Louisa F.
Kendall, M. F.
Kennoyer, W. W.
King, O. H.
Kimball, Sam H.
Knott, Harold E.
Kratz, David L.

L

Ladd, James Earl
La Dow, E. A.
Lane, E. Erie
Lattin, Grant F.
Law, O. J.
Leake, Ervin F.
Leavitt, Teddy
Leavitt, Linden
Leavitt, Maynard
Leggett, John F.

LeMasters, Clarence G.
Lemmon, W. S.
Lester, J. N.
Lewis, W. Ervin
Lindsay, W. A.
Linn, Andrew Fillmore
Lister, J. B.
Liveley, B. F.
Livingstone, Cassie D.
Livingstone, W. O.
Lobdell, G. L.
Lord, J. A.

M

MacDonald, Neil
MacDonald, Turner B.
Manning, W. M.
Marrs, W. P.
Martin, L. C.
Mathis, Charles R.
Matlock, Gareld L.
Matlock, W. T.
Maxey, R. Tibbs
McAllister, George H.
McBride, Dr. James
McCarty, A. V.
McCallum, Hugh N.
McCallum, James
McCallum, J. S.
McConnell, Howard
McConnell, J. N.
McCormick, W. F.
McCullough, W. L.
McIlvain, J. M.
McKeever, A. C.
McLean, A. I.
McQuary, Marion A.
McQueen, A. R.
McSparran, J. H.
Meisinger, George
Meldrum, A. McKenzie
Mell, Carman E.
Mellinger, Willard L.
Melton, J. A.
Messick, R. M.
Mick, Louis
Mick, Orville F.

Middleton, J. R.
Miles, Carl S.
Millard, D. E.
Miller, Byron F.
Moberg, James D.
Moomaw, Jacob
Moon, Everard R.
Moon, Rupert A.
Moore, Charles R.
Moore, J. D.
Moore, J. H.
Moralee, James
Morgan, Clarence C.
Morgan, D. Loyd
Morgan, George W.
Morgan, H. B.
Morgan, James E.
Morris, J. M.
Morris, Victor P.
Mortimore, Paul DeF.
Morton, R. L.
Mow, H. E.
Muckley, E. S.
Mulkey, A. H.
Mulkey, B. F.
Mulkey, I. N.
Mulkey, Philip
Murphey, John E.
Mussleman, Charles
Myers, Leon L.
Myers, Russell
Myers, Walter L.

N

Nahss, Charles T.
Nankivell, W. F.
Neal, B. M.
Neely, Claude J.
Nelson, Jerry
Newton, Lena E.
Norcross, David E.
Norcross, D. N.
Norris, B. F.
Nutting, David W.

O

Obert, Leslie
Olsen, R. N.

Olsen, David Eugene
Orrick, J. M.

P

Palmer, E. A.
Parker, Georgia
Parks, Glen
Parrish, Elery
Patterson, Elmer M.
Payne, Aaron
Peart, Isaac
Perkins, John Nelson
Petelle, Martin Luther
Peterson, Marion
Peterson, Orval D.
Petterson, Martin
Perry, H. Jackson
Phillips, Clifton A.
Phillips, C. H.
Picton, Thomas G.
Pierce, Frank L.
Piper, William C.
Pitman, W. B. F.
Pointer, James A.
Porter, F. T.
Porter, Leland W.
Porter, William
Powell, Alfred
Powell, John
Powell, L. Farris
Powell, Noah
Powell, P. O.
Price, Cedric
Proebstel, John E.
Pruitt, Veltie
Purcell, O. D.
Purnell, Frank Lewis
Putman, Melvin
Putnam, Edith
Putnam, Ralph L.

Q

Quill, A. W.

R

Radford, Charles T.
Radford, Thomas W.
Rambo, Kate

Rambo, W. E.
Ramsey, George H.
Ratcliffe, J. W.
Rawlings, T. W.
Read, T. L.
Reagor, W. F.
Reasoner, Norris J.
Reed, H. E.
Reeder, W. F.
Reid, T. P.
Reynolds, Clarence W.
Rice, Ward A.
Rice, Dallas
Richards, Charles H.
Richardson, C. F.
Richardson, George W.
Richardson, S. W.
Rickard, Dennis
Rickerson, Donald N.
Rigdon, John E.
Riggs, Barton Z.
Ritchey, George C.
Robb, W. E.
Robb, B. W. F.
Roberts, F. H.
Roberts, J. E.
Roberts, Carroll C.
Robinson, F. Elmo
Robinson, S. W.
Rose, Morton L.
Ross, Floyd A.
Ross, George A.
Rossell, H. E.
Ruble, William
Ruble, W. N.
Rowland, L. L.
Russell, F. E.
Ryder, H. E.

S

Sabin, Claude P.
Sadler, Lee
Sanderson, Eugene C.
Sawyer, R. H.
Scates, W. A.
Schmid, Gottlieb
Schoonover, Charles R.

Semones, William
Shaw, I. G.
Shaw, Roy
Shelley, J. M.
Shipp, C. H.
Shropshire, H. C.
Sias, Charles A.
Sias, C. Adrian
Sickafoose, K. H.
Simonds, George W.
Skaggs, A. D.
Sloan, Errol B.
Smith, C. P.
Smith, H. B.
Smith, J. N.
Smith, Raymond C.
Smith, W. M.
Snelling, Vincent
Snyder, Emery
Soward, E. L.
Spriggs, J. W.
Springer, George W.
Stanley, D. T.
Staley, R. A.
Stansbury, Howard
Stebbins, J. E.
Stephens, F. Claude
Stephens, L. F.
Stewart, J. F.
Stivers, Elijah V.
Stivers, John T.
Stivers, Lorraine
Stram, Walter E.
Straub, Walter L.
Stull, N. A.
Sunderman, A. H.
Sunkler, Lawrence
Sutherland, J.
Sutton, H. T.
Sutton, W. Phene
Swaim, W. D.
Swain, A. E.
Swander, Clarence F.
Sweaney, Elmer
Sweaney, A. M.
Swift, Elder

T

Taylor, Clive
Taylor, E. K.
Teel, I. H.
Thomas, Joyce H.
Thompson, Maynard B.
Thompson, M. J.
Thornton, C. L.
Thurston, Clyde C.
Titus, F. B.
Todd, A. L.
Tong, Lee
Toogood, Henry
Torgerson, Wilbur
Tout, J. F.
Trimble, C. F.
Trollinger, Elder
Tucker, Harry E.
Turner, M. J.
Tuttle, Harry

U

Underwood, P. P.
Utz, B. E.

V

Vail, Joel
Vallandingham, William N.
Van De Walker, J. W.
Van Slyke, A. F.
Van Winkle, Henry A.
Vaughn, David
Vernon, A. C.

W

Walker, O. A.
Walker, C. C.
Waller, H. M.
Ware, Elizabeth
Ware, Francis A.
Weaver, Tolbert F.
Weddle, E. E.
Welch, Philip
Wells, W. Lawrence
Wetzle, David

Whiddon, A. J.
Whipple, George R.
Whitaker, E. C.
White, Tilghman M.
White, J. C.
Whisler, Edwin
Whisler, Vivian
Wigmore, Ernest C.
Wilburn, James
Williams, George E.
Williams, Nelson O.
Williams, Otho
Williams, A. M.
Williamson, E. S.
Willis, H. L.
Wilson, W. Aubrey
Wilson, George
Wilson, William H.
Wiltse, W. H.
Wittkamper, J. W.
Wing, J. Orye

Wingo, Claude
Wolverton, Bruce
Wood, W. A.
Wood, Frank A.
Wood, Eldon L.
Workman, N. R.
Worstell, William C.
Word, Archie
Winder, Francis
Wright, Edward

Y

Young, A. W.
Young, John
Youtz, B. E.

Z

Zimmerman, George F.
Zook, Frank W.

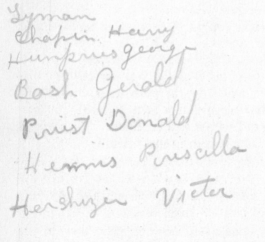

EPILOGUE

Finis must now be written. I have spent about seven years of research and writing upon this volume. I feel very much as I think I shall feel when I come to the end of the journey of life and review the deeds of my body. I can say in all truth that I have done the best that I could. But the deed is still imperfect. No one is more conscious of its imperfections than I. There are too many gaps to make it acceptable as a history. Early records were not kept—only fragments here and there were available from which to gather the data for a story. Some of these fragments were unreliable as was found from testing them with other facts. Some of them were conflicting in statement, and I am not at all sure that all the inaccuracies have been weeded out of the narrative. History should be accurate. Dates were particularly elusive. Places were known by different names at different times. Communities once prominent long ago have been deceased. Congregations have changed names and locations. The memory of the pioneers was no longer always reliable.

The study incident to this work has given me a more profound respect for the people known as Disciples of Christ than ever before. It has strengthened my faith in the fundamental position they occupy.

Very naturally I make no claim to originality in this work, except for the literary expression. I have gleaned from many sources, so that I cannot remember all. Among them I gladly acknowledge the following: Bound volumes of the *Millennial Harbinger* and *The Christian-Evangelist* in the Eugene Bible University library; old records and papers of the Oregon Christian Missionary Convention; a thesis on this same subject written by V. E. Hoven; private correspondence from J. V. Crawford, H. C. Porter, J. B. Lister, R. M. Messick, and many others; personal conversation with scores of pioneers and descendants of pioneers; books and histories of Oregon life too numerous to mention. To all everywhere who have furnished even the slightest information my sincere appreciation goes.

I sincerely hope that future historians will keep the work up-to-date, and may be able to correct the inaccuracies in this, so that in the far future generations yet unborn may be better informed as to our progress than we can possibly be of the progress of preceding generations. There is no more thrilling story in the world than the story of missionary and evangelistic progress. The glamour of the kingdom's advance is not confined to foreign lands, but there are plenty of thrilling tales of missionary service in the state of Oregon. These stories ought to inspire men and women to greater zeal and loyalty for pushing the borders of the kingdom outward and onward. It is in the hope that this volume may accomplish this in some degree that it is written. Did I not feel that it would do that I should never have undertaken the long weary hours at the typewriter that have been required. I shall have no jealousy in my soul should some future historian excel this work to a degree that it shall be overshadowed. Hoping that this work may inspire some one to make the attempt I gladly write the closing word.

FINIS